MY DEAR MOTHER

MY DEAR MOTHER

STORMY, BOASTFUL, AND TENDER

LETTERS BY DISTINGUISHED

SONS—FROM DOSTOEVSKY TO ELVIS

collected and annotated by
Karen Elizabeth Gordon and Holly Johnson

ALGONQUIN BOOKS OF CHAPEL HILL 1997

Published by
ALGONQUIN BOOKS OF CHAPEL HILL
Post Office Box 2225
Chapel Hill, North Carolina 27515-2225

a division of
WORKMAN PUBLISHING
708 Broadway
New York, New York 10003

Letters in this volume have been set as the originals, retaining idiosyncrasies in spelling and usage. Bracketed ellipses are used to indicate when material has been omitted by the editors.

Library of Congress Cataloging-in-Publication Data
My dear mother : stormy, boastful, and tender letters from distinguished sons—from Dostoevsky to
    Elvis / collected and annotated by Karen Elizabeth Gordon and Holly Johnson.
        p.   cm.
    Includes bibliographical references.
    ISBN 1-56512-121-X (hardcover)
    1. Artists—Correspondence. 2. Mothers and sons—Correspondence. 3. Arts.   I. Gordon,
    Karen Elizabeth. II. Johnson, Holly, 1943–.
NX90.M9   1997
700'.922
[B]—DC21   97-14494
                                                                                  CIP

10 9 8 7 6 5 4 3 2 1
First Edition

For Henri de Toulouse-Lautrec, our beloved inspiration,

and for our mothers, whose sons we are:

Camilla Honey Hall Collins and Anne Michalov Johnson

I'm beginning to think that the proper definition
of "Man" is "an animal that writes letters."

—LEWIS CARROLL

CONTENTS

III. YOUNG MAN

A Room of One's Own

Grand and Other Tours, with Gossip

Linen, Clothes, Evasions of Marriage, Elopements

ACKNOWLEDGMENTS

*F*or succor, support, hospitality and invaluable contributions, Holly Johnson wishes to thank Louise Boursua, the British School at Rome Library, William Donker, Suzanne Guest, the University of Bristol Library, the University of Bristol Art History Department, the Lewis and Clark College Library, Sacramento Rotary, Stanley Weintraub, Suzanne Nelson, Milo Radulovich, Darby Patterson, Philip Windwood, Marsha White, Brooks Koenig, and the staff at Il Fornaio Restaurant in Sacramento.

For help, encouragement, suggestions, hospitality, and multiform generosity, Karen Elizabeth Gordon offers thanks to: Danielle Mémoire and Guillaume Pineau des Forêts, Marisa Mascarelli, Hôtel des Grandes Ecoles, Alain Bloch, The American Library in Paris, Maia Gregory, Herbert Schimmel, Pat Nolan, Barbara Hodgson, Frank Marquardt, Grace Fretter, Steven Moore, Alba Witkin, Camilla Collins, Paul Walker, Peter Guralnick, Patroclos Stavrou, and Richard Press.

$\mathcal{W}$elcome to a drama of remarkable spirits revealed in an intimate setting. Absence is a muse for everyone present, including the book's creators, as the two of us were separated when the idea for *My Dear Mother* blazed before our eyes. Holly, studying art history at the University of Bristol, ran across the letters of Henri de Toulouse-Lautrec, as fresh as if they had been written yesterday. She sent them straightaway to Karen, who envisioned the book full-blown. Why not a cacophonous collection of letters from distinguished men to their mothers, and some mail from famous women in the arts to their sons as well?

And so they came in earnest, these letters, the correspondents growing from childhood into manhood, reversing roles with their mothers, while the two of us spanned the centuries and reversed continents. Holly returned to Portland, Oregon, and installed herself in the city library; Karen summoned her sources in Paris, clapping her hands and bringing forth a clatter of men of letters communing with their mothers. We encountered facets of artists, composers, and writers we thought we knew, and happened upon several total strangers. The delight of discovery that ignited this book sustained it all the way.

🌷

Between sons and mothers, neither has the last word. So they keep on writing when they can't be heard. (We must be thankful the telephone came along so late—how many of these letters would be lost, their words drawn down the phone lines and diffused into the atmosphere like smoke!) From tenderness to brutality, possessiveness to laissez-faire, the correspondence here touches a wide range of emotions on both sides of this inescapable bond, with its enduring tenacity.

Most men don't seem to mind their mother's solicitous questions and concern. Their responses, in fact, sound grateful: Ah, someone who really cares! They write of their doubts and defeats and obstacles, as well as their first earnings and honors in art, and announce their imminent rebellions. With one foot on the road to self-fulfillment, Gustave Courbet sells his school uniform and writes home: "If I'm to be an exception to every rule in every way, I'm off to pursue my destiny."

🌷

This collection celebrates the endless variations in love and affection such a pair may share—whether it's to ask for a favorite pair of socks or silk underwear, to suggest a change of linen, or to announce a recent coup or accomplishment. Pain and struggle are aired as well, sometimes with a demure request for a loan, backed up by a favorable prognosis: upcoming exhibitions, publications, some patron's promises or a critic's accolades. The tie that begins before birth may develop some troublesome knots and kinks. But however difficult the relationship, it somehow nourishes the creativity as it evolves through the years.

᷍

Letters catapult across great distances, from St.-John Perse in China to Paris and Flaubert in Egypt to Normandy—while Toulouse-Lautrec sends frequent loving, lively notes to his nearby *maman,* requesting truffles and capons and announcing his latest posters on the walls of Paris. In that city thirty-four years later, William Faulkner turns tenderhearted voyeur in the Luxembourg Gardens, his simple words a striking contrast to the pompous, contrived aria of praise that Richard Wagner composes to his *Mutter.* Letters in the "Grand Tour" chapter trace the travels of Joseph Spence, Alexander Pope's protégé; Beat writer Jack Kerouac in search of postwar America; and Tennessee Williams tasting Paris—and champagne—for the first time, at seventeen. Little Balzac, away at school, is banished to the alcove, while Baudelaire the teenager discloses with unembellished candor: "You want to know my grades. I have bad news for you." (Decades later, Baudelaire has other chagrining news to share: his hair has gone quite white.) In the midst of his elopement, Shelley requests his Galvanic Machine and Solar Microscope. Henry James steals away from an opulent gathering to commune with his fireplace and his mammy. Nikos Kazantzakis, with his great, generous spirit, looks "like a grassy meadow" in an all-green getup as he strolls through Florence and straight into our hearts.

Mothers, too, make dramatic appearances. Vanessa Bell shows up in mustachioed drag, slipping into her son Quentin's skin and seeing the world through a man's eyes at a gender-switching masquerade ball. George Sand, a political animal dressed notoriously in trousers, lords over her Lord-Mayor son Maurice with, "Ho, ho, Mr. Mayor, you had better step carefully." From her South American tour, Sarah Bernhardt's exotic epic letter of shipwreck, puma hunt, and baccarat game reads like a glorious bedtime story.

Voices rise and fall. Along with the scratch of quills, the clack of typewriters, the rustle of a silk dressing gown comes a whisper, then mumblings, followed by entreaties, boasting, and verbal caresses between sons and their mothers. The volume grows. Sentences spill over the decades. Paragraphs leap across time and fall over each other in letters, telegrams, and postcards. From closets and courtyards, from ship cabins and army tents, from bedsides and boudoirs they come, intimations and confessions next to laundry lists, prolix descriptions of strange lands and experiences besides bleats of joy or anguish. With letters from sons outnumbering those of mothers, "We are up to our ears in Boydom," to borrow George Eliot's words, and soon, dear reader, shall you be.

MY DEAR MOTHER

Boy

OH! MUMMIE
WHAT A LIFE

e. e. cummings

and I will send an elephant to baby sister

AUBREY BEARDSLEY

When is my engine going to be mended?

HENRI DE TOULOUSE-LAUTREC

your boy who kisses you 1000000000000000 times

HONORÉ DE BALZAC

I do not forget to clean my teeth with my handkerchief

BENJAMIN BRITTEN

arn't we an industrious family of immortles

F. SCOTT FITZGERALD

Please send me a dollar [. . .] I will spend it causiusly

EZRA POUND

the umpire cheated until pa come and then he quit

WYNDHAM LEWIS

I must say (the fellows will talk) Goodbye

e. e. cummings (1894–1962)

e. e. cummings, American poet and playwright (the play him *involved a mother's delivery and questionable paternity), was already fusing words and images in the letters he wrote at the age of eight.*

[135 Nahant St.
April 23, 1902]

Dear Mother
I hope that you and the baby are all very well are they? I will send a lion to you and I will send an elephant to baby sister. We have duck's eggs for breakfast they are very good and I wish that you would have some. Wont we have a nice time up at the farm.

With love
Estlin

My cold is better

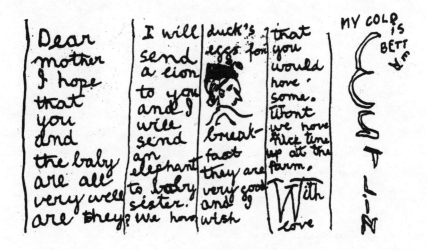

AUBREY BEARDSLEY *(1872–1898)*

A weakness in his lungs (which remained, and later directed him away from music, talented and taken with both it and theatricals though he was) put letter-crossing distance between seven-year-old Aubrey Beardsley and his mother: he was sent to a small boarding school near Brighton, whence this letter was sent. The chinoiserie fad that later may have influenced his drawings came early to him here, with frequent outings to the Chinese Gardens, for romps and such noted occasions as a Temperance Fete. In another letter, the future eroticist reports an early artistic collaboration: gathering moss to decorate the Church for Easter. He would grow into erotica later. We must treasure these precious moments with him; at the age of seven, he was already through more than a quarter of his life, which, though brief, so marked his time that it took his name: the Beardsley Era.

Thursday [6 November 1879]
Hamilton Lodge

My dear Mother,

Thank you for sending my shirts. Last Saturday we all went to see the wedding of one of the boy's sisters. We had a large cake sent us. The Saturday before we went to a Circus. I liked it very much. There were two large Elephants who did all kinds of funny things. Last night Miss Wise let us make a bonfire in the playground, and then the boys let off some fireworks. We had great fun and stayed up a little later than usual. I am quite well and happy. Please send me some more money, mine is nearly gone, and all the boys give one or two shillings towards the expenses of the play, which they act at the break-up party. When is my engine going to be mended? Give my love to father and Mabel and yourself.

Your loving son AUBREY

HENRI DE TOULOUSE-LAUTREC *(1864–1901)*

Postimpressionist painter of the Parisian dance halls, brothels, and cabarets, Henri was the center of Countess Adèle de Toulouse-Lautrec's life. She went so far as to wear him: she had a ring made from Henri's first four baby teeth. Cloyingly devout, she was devoted to her son, whose God-given talents were evident from his earliest drawings, radiant with his wit: dogs wearing spurs and dressed as boys, or bearing arms; goats, monkeys, costumed riders on horseback or astride dogs; and the family priest with the head of a dog smoking a pipe. This letter was written by the boy Henri in English to exercise his foreign language. The postscripted allusion to drowning must indicate that his ma was at the spa, as she often was—sometimes accompanied by Henri, treating his stunted legs.

Neuilly 22

Septembre 75

My dear Mamma,

I was very glad of receiving such a pretty letter and I will tell you very good news. My Greek master was very satisfied with me and he put on a piece of paper "I am very satisfied of the lessons as well of the tasks." He gave me a Latin version to do. I have read my Latin Grammar this morning and I am going to do Miss' tasks. Yesterday I went to the bath and I have looked for the plate. M. Verrier was very satisfied with my legs. When you will return I hope you will find me well. Give my love to every one and return soon. If I had wings I should go to see you but I have no. I finish my letter by telling you that everybody send you his compliments and particularly your boy who kisses you 1000000000000000 times.

Your affectionate boy, Coco de Lautrec

My kiss

P.S. Don't drawn you or send me a telegram

HONORÉ DE BALZAC *(1799–1850)*

The *"alcove"* referred to in this earliest letter by Balzac is really a miniature dungeon beneath the stairs, a schoolboy's oubliette, in the dormitory at Vendôme. Over the course of six years, his mother visited young Balzac but twice, although most of his schoolmates' parents showed up regularly for prize giving, and gave their sons pocket money, which Honoré's mother never did, leaving him without funds for the games and treats his schoolfellows enjoyed. Balzac was always painfully aware of his mother's preference for her other, illegitimate son, and wrote repeatedly of mothers adoring their adulterated offspring in his great sprawling series of novels, The Human Comedy. The *"accessit"* Balzac mentions here refers to a consolation prize for speech in Latin, in this case a history of Charles XII of Sweden, the volume bound in rough sheepskin and inscribed in gold lettering: "prix à Honoré Balzac, 1808."

Vendôme
1 May [1808]

My dear Mother,

    I think Papa was very unhappy when he heard that I had been put in the alcove. To console him please tell him that I have got an *accessit*. I do not forget to clean my teeth with my handkerchief. I have a new exercise-book in which I make fair copies of my exercises and I get good marks and that is how I hope to please you. I embrace you warmly and all the family and the gentlemen of my acquaintance [...]

Balzac Honorés,
Your obedient and affectionate son.

BENJAMIN BRITTEN *(1913–1976)*

What British composer Benjamin Britten lacked in spelling skills he made up for in expressivity, as this letter, written in his tenth year, reveals. It describes a life busy with household members, teachers, friends, and music studies. The words here tumble out, phoneticized, as if their sounds were more important than spelling, as if the musicality of words, no matter how oddly spelled, were essentially what mattered.

21, Kirkley Cliff Road, Lowestoft

November 7th, 1923.

My Mummie darling,

Oh! Mummie what a life, (!) a piece of news was given to me this morning by Miss Ethel——My Exam (Thery) is on the 12th wednesday Next and you wont be home, I suppose it would be noosty of me to ask you to be home, so I wont but oh! I wish you could be. The zam is at 2 till five' W've got to be there at a quarter to 2. Dummy! [. . .] "Lazy" said that she'd take me out on Sunday with Duffer. Rosie is stoneing raisens (but I've eaten more than she's stoned). She's just put the raisan in the cup (for pips) and pips in the bigone. Pounder has just lent me a story about nice bugalers and murderers called Raffles 6d edition. Alice is sewing and so's Mary, I'm writing as you see, so arn't we an industrious family of ~~kittens~~ immortles. I hope you arrived safely and did Bobby meet you on the Stamford road? I hope the car ran well, and you did not run over any bodie, (or doggie) [. . .] My music lessen went quite well this morning I did all thery and no playing. Miss Ethel said that she'd send me down and other paper to work. I am going to have a lesson on Miss Ethel's piano, and I am only to take my exam list and scales so Heaven only knows when I'm to do my paper because I've got to show it up on Monday and to-day's Friday. I shall have to go to bed in a minute so I can't say Much more. By-the-way when you are going to Beth, please let me know when because I'll want to write to you.

With tons and cwts. and lbs. and ozs. of pakages of Love,

You own tiny little (sick-for-Muvver)

BENI

Michelangelo's mother, Francesca, sent him off to be raised by a wet nurse when he was a baby. It just so happened that the wet nurse's husband and father were both stonemasons. Years later the great sculptor jokingly said that he had taken up the hammer and chisel along with her milk.

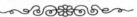

F. SCOTT FITZGERALD *(1896–1940)*

Author of "The Diamond as Big as The Ritz," Tender Is the Night, *and* The Great Gatsby, *Fitzgerald, whose adult life on the Continent would be notoriously fast and flashy, is characteristically concerned about pocket money as he writes home from summer camp.*

To: Mollie McQuillan Fitzgerald

Summer 1907

Camp Chatham. Orillia, Ontario

Dear Mother,

I wish you would send me five dollars as all my money is used up. Yesterday I went in a running contest and won a knife for second prize. This is a picture of Tom Penney and I starting on a paper chase.

Your loving son

Scott Fitzgerald

Either he went through the five dollars in a hurry or never received it, as this second request for money implies:

July 18, 07

Dear Mother, I recieved your letter this morning and though I would like very much to have you up here I dont think you would like it as you know no one hear except Mrs. Upton and she is busy most of the time I dont think you would like the accomadations as it is only a small town and no good hotels. There are some very nise boarding houses but about the only fare is lamb and beef. Please send me a dollar becaus there are a lot of little odds and ends i need. I will spend it causiusly. All the other boys have pocket money besides their regullar allowence.

Your loving son
Scott Fitzgerald

. . . How beautiful your mother was, how pale,
When so tall and so languid, stooping,
she straightened your heavy hat of straw or of sun,
lined with a double seguine leaf,
and when, piercing a dream to shadows consecrated,
the dazzle of muslin
inundated your sleep!

—St.-John Perse
"To Celebrate a Childhood"

EZRA POUND *(1885–1972)*

American poet and critic Ezra Pound, whose mother appears formal and stiff in the multicultural world of his crowning work, the Cantos, *wrote this letter to her while she was visiting her family in New York. Pound would later turn his eccentric spelling into a stylistic flourish, inventing his own word forms and escaping the rigors of standard orthography.*

Wyncote
Oct 1. 1895

Dear Ma,

    I went to a ball game on Saturday between our school and the Heacocks. the score was thirty-five to thirty-seven our favor, it was a hard fight in which wee were victorise. They put in a colored man for first base and then to pitcher but he soon was knock out as he gave two many men laces on balls, as it did not do any good they chucked him off, the umpire cheated until pa come and then he quit he was accused of being bulyed into it by the heacocks who it is sed paid him but he denies it.

    Wee spent a pleasant sunday. Monday I went after wlnuts and picked for Dayton and Fousty as I could not cary hom all I picked up and so I now have a flourbag full. To day I went for chestnuts, but got not enough to speak of (I went with Tom and Pud) then went up to Puds where wee met Joe and then wee played fussy untill I had to go hom. Wee are well and happy give my love to aunt Frank and Cousin Sady. As nobody has looked over this pleas excuse mistakes.

Love from all
Your loving son
E. L. Pound

When Julio Cortázar (1914–1984), the Argentine short-story magician and innovative novelist (Hopscotch, 62: A Model Kit), was sixty-seven, his wife, Carol Dunlop, reported that his mother was still fussing about his Levi's and the length of his hair. In a 1983 interview with Jason Weiss, Cortázar unfurls the following story of how his mother cultivated his imagination—further than she meant it to go.

JW: What interested you about the fantastic in the beginning? Were you very young?

JC: Oh yes. It began with my childhood. I was very surprised, when I was going to grade school, that most of my young classmates had no sense of the fantastic. They were very realistic. They took things as they were . . . that's a plant, that's an armchair. And I was already seeing the world in a way that was very changeable. For me things were not so well defined in that way, there were no labels. My mother, who is a very imaginative woman, helped me a lot. Instead of telling me, "No, no, you should be serious," she was pleased that I was very imaginative, and when I turned toward the world of the fantastic, she helped me because she gave me books to read. That's how at the age of nine I read Edgar Allan Poe for the first time. That book I stole because my mother didn't want me to read it, she thought I was too young and she was right. The book scared me and I was ill for three months, because I believed in it.

W Y N D H A M L E W I S *(1884–1957)*

British painter and novelist Percy Wyndham Lewis, who dropped his first name when his voice changed, was born on his father's yacht, so his first feel of life was not such a jolt from the safe harbor of his mother's womb. They did share a rare trust and closeness; perhaps these gentle beginnings rocked them into a peaceable future. Here, in describing his fellow classmates, we hear the beginnings of the voice and blared opinions that would inaugurate Vorticism— Lewis's vital version of Futurism—in his revolutionary review, BLAST.

County School, Bedford
[1894]

My dear Mother.

I hope you are quite well. I am having a very good time indeed. I am in the third form, I hope I shall soon be in the fourth. I got an exit to go in the town yesterday and fooled about the whole afternoon, while Marshall secundus and Madame Mildred (Waldram) went up the river in a boat (Farrar wont let me, I can't swim). Marshall is a nice chap, but a deuce of a prig. Waldram is all right. Micaule or Butcher is head prefect. He is not the oldest chap in the school only being about 18. Jones is not a bad fellow, but a deuce of a fool. Thorpe sextus is an ass too. Mansell Jones is a fine fellow. So's Boby Clarke, a chap of about sixteen, I work with. I say, there are a lot of big fellows in our form. It is nearly eleven, and I must say (the fellows will talk) Goodbye.

Your very loving son,
P. Lewis

*I*n the following year, Lewis writes to his mother of getting on very well with his wood carving, and obtaining permission to practice it in the playground shed—already taking on hard surfaces and playing with form, as he would do later, founding the Rebel Art Centre and the Vorticist movement in London with Ezra Pound.

ADOLESCENT

OUT OF THE NEST

WALLACE STEVENS

I can be your own dearest tootsey wootsey

JOHN DOS PASSOS

We are within thine ancient walls!

WYNDHAM LEWIS

I've never had a more exciting twenty minutes than that cab drive

VICTOR HUGO

we are quite lost

EVELYN WAUGH

The whole day seems different

TENNESSEE WILLIAMS

this Biltmore bed looks as seductive as Paradise to the damned

WOLFGANG AMADEUS MOZART

I had a great desire today to ride on a donkey

WILLIAM CARLOS WILLIAMS

about halfway round the room I started to walk up the front of her dress

WALLACE STEVENS *(1879–1955)*

"And of the fragrant mothers the most dear"
—"To the One of Fictive Music"

Correspondence was to become a rich source of the strange and distant, complementing Steven's idiosyncratic and exotic vocabulary, as his muse leapt to his side, becoming his dearest tootsey wootsey (an offbeat closing the American poet uses here to tickle his mother) through his prolific decades as a poet.

Rarely leaving Hartford and his crisply tailored legal vocation in an insurance company, yet always longing to go to Europe, Stevens engaged in correspondence as one way of feeding his imagination, requesting of various far-flung friends Ceylon tea or French art catalogs. As one of his letters says: "It means a lot to me to know a man in Dublin, to receive letters from a friend in Italy, to look at the map of Spain . . . " These fragments infused Stevens's poetry with landscape, fragrance, and pictures—although his late poetry returned to his boyhood and youth and was populated by figures resembling his own parents, rather than by the fops, clowns, and dandies of his earlier poems.

[Ephrata, Pa.]
July-23—1895

My Dear Mother—
    I write this letter in depressed spirits. I have decided to come home. Ephrata as a summer resort is still extant as a pleasure resort is dead, very dead, indeed, or has my cynicism embittered me. [. . .] I can go either with 20 to 25 year old fellows who of course regard it as condescension or 11 to 14 lads who regard it as an ascension [. . .] There are none on the same build as Wallace Stevens except perhaps two [,] one of whom is [a] damned ass and the other a G— D— one. Both their precious skulls have been permeated with fascinations of the ladies—I hate ladies? (such as are here)[.] [They] are all agreeable enough but familiarity breeds contempt [. . .] I have practically lost appetite or become hungered at the most Godless hours of the night. I ate for my morning's meal a little oatmeal—two tiny little saucers, I did not go down to dinner hoping thus to add a stimulus to supper, which consisted of some unnameable smathering of greasy fritters, a measly plate of measly beef and of course the inevitable applesauce. [. . .] If Reading were as miserable as Ephrata I should be solaced in a measure but I can at least swim in clean, clear, wet water, I can eat food, I can swear when ever the eloquence of boiling passion rises, I can use both eyes when looking, I can contract debts, I can be your own dearest tootsey wootsey—.
                                        [Wallace?] Stevens—H

JOHN DOS PASSOS *(1896–1970)*

To create a backdrop for the book, American novelist John Dos Passos scattered newspaper headlines throughout his sprawling political trilogy, U.S.A., a patchwork of narrative, news stories, songs, and more. His use of short fragmented announcements, like trumpet calls, resonate with wit in an early postcard from Italy that he wrote to his mother, whom he teasingly dubbed the Princess.

[Rome
December 14, 1911]

Imperial Rome!
Conqueror of the world!
Enlightener of the ages!
We are within thine ancient walls!
From the Imperial City to the Royal Princess love and greeting
I will write to Her sublime, serene and celestial majesty tomorrow.
With much love from her
Jack—

I wanted to say that my talent lay hidden somewhere in her, that through her everything had been passed on to me, everything except her spirit. [. . .]

"Look, Mama, do you like it?"

She looks at my painting with God only knows what eyes! I await the verdict. At last she says slowly:

"Yes, my son, I see; you have talent. But, my child, listen to me. Perhaps it would be better for you to be a clerk. I'm sorry for you. Where do you get that in our family?"

—Marc Chagall

WYNDHAM LEWIS *(1884–1957)*

After his parents' separation, Lewis was left with every boy's dream: his lovely mother all to himself. They lived in a movable household within or near London, his resourceful mother supporting him while Wyndham, as he was called, often at the bottom of his class, attended private schools—until he enrolled in the Slade School of Art and began distinguishing himself, as he would later in both art and literature. It is palpably evident in all his letters to his mother that Lewis enjoyed an exceptionally close and affectionate friendship with her, sharing confidences and perplexities, artistic aspirations and romantic ambivalences, and a great deal of ironic humor directed at himself and the world in which he moved.

> 92 Calle Mayor Tercero. c/o Mrs. Briggs.
> [Madrid]
> [1902?]

Chere Maman. . . .

Gore and I have got a Studio for which we pay about 4/6 a week each: we bought some things for it, which we can sell again for half I suppose when we leave. [. . .] We wanted to know about models etc. and wanted to get a studio and not waste time, so Mrs. Briggs said she knew of a man who would help us: he's been as quick as a Spaniard could be and got us settled in our studio, bought our furniture cheap, and got us any amount of models, and been very helpful [. . .]

> Sunday

Since writing the above several days have elapsed. [. . .] The Prado is a very wonderful place: we got shown yesterday the room of Goya drawings:

We also visited an artist, (ridiculous person) and to do so hired a conveyance: I've never had a more exciting twenty minutes than that cab drive: we had our side-step smashed by a carriage, and stopped the traffic several times, quarrelled with everybody; were turned out of main street for frightening a mule-team and using bad language: dived into dark narrow lane, and finding large cart facing us, turned round, having first driven on to pavement, and nearly into shop-window: we reached the artist at last, and found him, as I said, a ridiculous person. [...]

With love etc.

I am,

PERCY W. LEWIS

VICTOR HUGO *(1802–1885)*

The famous French novelist, whose books present the dire condition of France's lower class in such turbulent blockbusters as Les Misérables *and* The Hunchback of Notre Dame, *sounds like a real mama's boy in this letter. His plaintive cry, "Mamma, mamma," resembles a voice, très misérable, in the wilderness. The same voice, as an adult, would turn into a battle cry of revolution uttered through the mouths of his heroic protagonists.*

[To Madame la Comtesse Hugo, at Thionville]
2d August, 1815.

MY DEAR MAMMA,—We are very dull here since you left. We often go to see M. Foucher, as you told us to do. He proposed to us to join in the lessons his sons are taking; we thanked him and declined. Every morning we work at Latin and mathematics. A letter with a black seal, and addressed to Abel, came the evening you went away. M. Foucher will send it on to you. He was kind enough to take us to the museum. . . . Come home soon. We don't know what to say or do without you; we are quite lost. We are always thinking of you. Mamma, mamma!

Your dutiful son,
VICTOR

Evelyn Waugh (1903–1966)

Evelyn Waugh, the English novelist whose Brideshead Revisited *explores family relationships and the effects of a rather toxic mother (and whose funnier* Vile Bodies *spoofs high society with a generous garnish of black humor), remembered his own maternal parent, Catherine Waugh, as "small, neat, reticent, and until her last decade, very active. She had no special literary interests, but read a book a fortnight, always a good one . . . I associate her less with lillies than with earthy wash-leather gloves and baskets of globe artichokes and black and red currants."*

[To Catherine Waugh]
[6 December 1920]

Darling Mother,

I have just heard from father about your illness. I can't say how sorry I am. The whole day seems different. We are having the concert this afternoon and I am hoping to see Barbara but it all seems meaningless now.

It was awfully kind of you to keep it from me until now. I do wish I was able to come and see you, dear. It does seem so far away. Do get well quickly—I shall be back in ten days now.

Your very loving,
Evelyn

TENNESSEE WILLIAMS *(1911–1983)*

Unlike Catherine Holly, his tortured heroine in Suddenly, Last Summer
*who goes off to Paris and other European hotspots with her suave cousin
Sebastian to unwittingly procure boyfriends for him, Southern playwright
Tennessee was bright-eyed and innocent when he traveled away from home
the summer when he was seventeen. Touring with his grandfather, young Tom
went in style, hobnobbing with the elite and gushing forth the rich details of
each day to his mother, Edwina, in letters, these two from New York and Paris.
The wry humor that would later surface in Williams's heart-wrenching plays
inspired by family members percolates joyfully in these lighthearted
communications.*

Dear Mother,
I am dead tired! It is after eleven o'clock and this Biltmore bed
looks as seductive as Paradise to the damned. . . . We have just
concluded dinner with a multi-millionaire, one of Mrs. Watson's
partners, in his seven room suite at the end of the hall. Dinner
served in princely style by the foreign waiter!
Grandfather is perfectly thrilled. And of course I am! This man
is a partner of *Wrigley's*. The first thing he did was to offer us some
chewing gum. Tomorrow morning Grandfather and I are to have
our breakfasts served in our room. At noon we meet Mrs. Watson
and motor out to her magnificent country Estate. In the evening
we attend a performance of The Show Boat. . . .
Also Mrs. Watson has assured Grandfather that if Gov. Al Smith,
who rooms at the Biltmore at present, comes here, she will give
Grandfather an introduction. Really, I wouldn't be a bit surprised if
Mrs. W. K. Vanderbilt didn't call at the door this next instant!

What almost knocked me over during the dinner was when Mr. Cummings told me that I was sitting at the same table, in his private suite, where the Prince of Wales had sat during his stay at the Biltmore in 1921!! Did that kill me!

Mrs. Watson is a lovely woman but I've never known anyone to talk with the rapidity that she does. She can't seem to get the words out of her mouth fast enough to suit her. . . . Well, we had a perfectly splendid trip up here on the train. I wish I could tell you all the things we're going to do here, but I don't know myself yet. Tomorrow morning Grandfather and I are going to do a little excursioning on our own—around the Main Blvds, on the buses, etc.

In the meantime, the strongest smelling salts couldn't keep me awake.

Love to all,
Tom

Paris
le 19 Juillet

Dear Mother,

I have just imbibed a whole glass of french champagne and am feeling consequently very elated. It is our last evening in Paris which excuses the unusual indulgence. French champagne is the only drink that I like here. But it is really delicious.

We have certainly had an exciting time in Paris. We've done practically everything there is to do. Today we went to the Louvre and out to Versailles. . . . We stood upon the balcony upon which Marie Antoinette boldly faced the mob which came to threaten her life. We looked into the secret passageway through which she fled when the crowd of enraged citizens broke into her boudoir.

The palace is exquisite throughout. All the ceilings are covered with rich paintings—the walls inlaid with gold. We walked down the long hall of mirrors, with its resplendent chandeliers and windows opening out upon the beautifully landscaped garden. It is the room in which the peace treaty of the Great War was signed. We saw the very table it was signed upon.

What appealed to me the most was the park in which Marie Antoinette found retreat from the court life which she detested. It was in this park that she played milk-maid. We saw . . . the huge, gold carriages in which she rode on fete days. [. . .]

We have seen the two notorious Parisian shows—The Folies Bergere and the Moulin Rouge. They both completely live up to their reputation. No American show would dare to put over the things that they did. It was, however, more artistic than it was immodest. Anyway, when you're in Paris, you might as well leave all dispensable conventions behind. I can easily see why some people look upon Paris as the whole world. It really is marvelous. [. . .]

Wolfgang Amadeus Mozart *(1756–1791)*

Celestial wunderkind, naughty Austrian boy, composer of divertimenti, concertos, quartets, symphonies, and operas—including The Marriage of Figaro, Don Giovanni, Così fan Tutte, *and* The Magic Flute—*Mozart spent less time with his mother than with his father, Leopold, who traveled throughout Europe with the child prodigy, amazing noble ears wherever he went. When little Wolfie played for the Empress Maria Theresa in Vienna, he leaped into her lap and asked her for a kiss. Mozart tacked this carefree message onto correspondence to his mother from Papa Leopold, conveniently tucking in the last word before the letter was sealed.*

[Bologna]

[21 August 1770]

I too am still alive and, what is more, as merry as can be. I had a great desire to-day to ride on a donkey, for it is the custom in Italy, and so I thought that I too should try it. We have the honour to go about with a certain Dominican, who is regarded as a holy man. For my part I do not believe it, for at breakfast he often takes a cup of chocolate and immediately afterwards a good glass of strong Spanish wine; and I myself have had the honour of lunching with this saint who at table drank a whole decanter and finished up with a full glass of strong wine, two large slices of melon, some peaches, pears, five cups of coffee, a whole plate of cloves and two full saucers of milk and lemon. He may, of course, be following some sort of diet, but I do not think so, for it would be too much; moreover he takes several little snacks during the afternoon. Addio. Farewell. [. . .]

WILLIAM CARLOS WILLIAMS *(1883–1963)*

Even though the waltz might have gotten away from American poet William Carlos Williams, words didn't. They ran and skipped his way, they danced circles around him. With a stethoscope in one hand and a pen in the other, Williams balanced a career as a physician with the life of a poet, although at nineteen, he couldn't keep his balance on the dance floor.

[University of Pennsylvania]
[Dec. 9, 1902]

My dear Mother: We have been having awful weather here . . . I went to the dance . . . and I certainly was glad I had a dress suit, for every other fellow there had one. . . . I went downstairs and was introduced to about fifteen young ladies. Of course I asked each one for a dance and trusted to luck to determine whether they knew how or not. . . . I had the first dance with Miss Ecob. It was a two-step, and I got along all right but next came a waltz. Oh, boy! I don't know who my partner was but I do know that she can't dance the waltz. We started. At the first step I knew something was wrong; about halfway round the room I started to walk up the front of her dress. I descended hurriedly and excused myself as best I could. We started again. Pretty soon she started on a journey up my leg. This was too much for me and I backed out. As I went upstairs for repairs I saw her contemplating me with a sad, disgusted look on her face. After this I sat out all the waltzes. Not a single person there knew how to dance a waltz. . . . After a while I began to get acquainted and just then everybody went home. My only regret is that now I have started I may be invited to more dances and it is either a case of refusing or finding a gold mine somewhere. I don't like these kind of dances much, because they are too formal. The people I met are too sporty for me.

Love and kisses to you, papa, and Ed from your loving son.

WILLIE

*M*any years and a marriage later, Williams found the perfect dance partner in the silence of the night, and sang his praises in the poem "Danse Russe":

If I when my wife is sleeping
and the baby and Kathleen
are sleeping
and the sun is a flame-white disc
in silken mists
above shining trees,—
if I in my north room
dance naked, grotesquely
before my mirror
waving my shirt round my head
and singing softly to myself:
"I am lonely, lonely.
I was born to be lonely,
I am best so!"
If I admire my arms, my face,
my shoulders, flanks, buttocks
against the yellow drawn shades,—

Who shall say I am not
the happy genius of my household?

SCHOOL DAYS

GUSTAVE COURBET

If I'm to be an exception to every rule in every way,
I'm off to pursue my destiny

NIKOS KAZANTZAKIS

And I'll go to the best dancing school in Athens

CHARLES BAUDELAIRE

You want to know my grades. I have bad news for you

A. E. HOUSMAN

Nothing very remarkable has happened

IVAN TURGENEV'S MOTHER

You are the one who hurts me most

DANTE GABRIEL ROSSETTI

I have nearly finished studying the bones

FYODOR DOSTOEVSKY

I am overcome by such sadness

E. B. WHITE

It is time, so I see, for my mid-week's effusion

GEORGE ELIOT TO HER STEPSON

our muscles are much astonished at the unusual exercise

GUSTAVE COURBET *(1819–1877)*

Painter, iconoclast, and enfant terrible *of Parisian society, Gustave Courbet is already delightfully willful, ready to strike out on his own, when he writes this letter home at the age of eighteen.*

[Besançon]
[November 30, 1837]

Dear family:

Perhaps you think that what I wrote you was a joke. Not at all, for I have already sold my school uniform for thirty-eight francs, after the tailor told me it was worth thirty-five. I absolutely want to leave my classes for I'm here perforce. I no longer ask to be in town, or even less to be in school, but only to be taken out. For that matter, the headmaster gave me two weeks to get adjusted. Write and ask him to return your money. As for me, if you insist on forcing me to stay, I will soon no longer be here.

I was touched by the letter you wrote me, but I cannot stay, no matter what. Besides, if I stayed I would be losing a year and you would be losing one thousand francs. You might as well throw them in the water. Since I have been here, I have not yet opened a book. I cannot do a thing, no one gives a damn about me anywhere, everyone tells me I cannot keep up. [. . .] If I'm to be an exception to every rule in every way, I'm off to pursue my destiny.

Write me as soon as possible what you have decided, for my stay here is costing me a great deal, especially as I am not doing anything.

I embrace you with all my heart. [. . .] I would like to be able to stay here to please you but I cannot.

Gustave Courbet

NIKOS KAZANTZAKIS *(1885–1957)*

Beloved by free spirits around the world, Greek author Nikos Kazantzakis wrote Zorba the Greek *and* The Greek Passion *(in which villagers putting on a play about Christ end up playing their theatrical parts in real life amid local political strife). His wife, Helen Kazantzakis, who created a biography based on his letters, writes: "With his mother and his sisters, whom he adored, he adopted a bantering tone, . . . teasing them each in turn, paying them compliments, offering them advice and little gifts, searching for powders and ribbons for them, and even a corset. . . . He spent his holidays in Crete. He needed to be close to his mother in order to replenish his strength." The following letter is from his university days in Athens.*

[Athens]
[1904]

Dearest Mother, Anestasia and Eleni,

I am very, very happy with our housekeeping. [. . .] When we get back from the university, we dash right over to the pot. I take the lid off and sniff, while the other two stand over me asking, "Did it turn out right? How did you find it?"

I taste two or three forkfuls, pretend to think it over, and if I'm hungry I tell them, "Disgusting!" (So I can tell Angeliki to put more on my plate without the others starting a brawl.)

I've got them on a diet. Every day I want vegetables. "Look here," they say to me, "won't you get some meat just once? We'll forget what it's like."

"Meat?" I ask them. "Meat? You know what illnesses it causes? You know there's no more dangerous food? So you want us to get sick?" . . .

How I wish it were possible for us all to be in Athens together, and you could stay here ten days or so to see what the world really means.

Perhaps this will happen. For, as I see [the following to his sisters] progress is being made—since you are learning to dance now. So you know the polka perfectly! Bravo! But don't neglect your French. And I'll go to the best dancing school in Athens. [. . .]

CHARLES BAUDELAIRE (1821–1867)

Long before he was sent off to school—with the arrival of his stepfather, Monsieur Aupick—Baudelaire became bereft of the world of his childhood, which was suffused with sensual impressions that nourished this aesthete par excellence. "Genius is only childhood rediscovered at will," he later wrote, and his poetry did return to those early sensations, recapturing the lost Eden so headily described in a letter to a friend in 1860:

> . . . the child is caressed, unbeknownst to women, by all the grace of a woman. So he loves his mother, his sister, his wet nurse, for the agreeable brush of satin and furs, for the smell of the bosom and the hair, for the click of the jewelry, for the play of ribbons, for all this world of femininity, which begins with the chemise and is even reflected in the furniture on which woman leaves the imprint of her sex.

Although Charles Baudelaire's later letters swerve wildly from one extreme to another in his feelings toward his mother, his letters from school are often untrammeled in affection and appreciation.

[June 1838]

My dear mother, I have just received your letter; if you knew how happy I am when you tell me that you think of me all the time, that you are always concerned about me, that I must work hard, and distinguish myself! You call that your refrain; I've heard you say that it must be tedious to hear you repeat the same thing over and over. Not at all! Your advice gives me the greatest pleasure. Could it be that, not having heard it for some time, it seems pleasantly new? Or perhaps in their solicitude mothers have a talent for expressing the same ideas over and over, but with a new style that makes them seem fresh. This may sound frivolous, but after all, why couldn't it be true?

You want to know my grades. I have bad news for you: I am fourteenth in Latin translation. The passage was taken from a very obscure and very bad author. M. Rinn told me laughing, and as if to console me, that one should almost feel proud not to understand those writers, because they are so ridiculous. He is always kind, sympathetic. I am delighted and I congratulate myself for having *once* met a teacher I like. Recently, exasperated by my chatting, he punished me and told me at the end of the class: "Baudelaire, you must really be unsatisfied with me, your homework is poor today and I have put you on detention." I replied that, because he is so kind, I couldn't allow myself to be irritated when he punished me. And then when he said: "Believe me, it is difficult to punish one's friends," I replied: "After what you have said, punishment cannot be painful." M. Rinn is the only teacher to whom I say things like that without blushing. With someone else I would be ashamed to utter such cheap flattery, but one is never ashamed to be honest with people one cares for. That is why, no matter what you say, one is never afraid to kiss one's mother, even in a crowded visiting room.

This is my life now: I read the books I am allowed to take from the library, I study, and I write poetry, but at the moment it is terrible. In spite of all this I am bored. The principal reason—there are others—is that I never see you. The conversations we have here in school are often meaningless and very boring; and so I frequently leave my friends, sometimes to go for a walk by myself, sometimes to try other company and other conversation. These frequent

absences offend my friends, and so as not to hurt them even more,
I have gone back to them; but our conversation is nothing but
chit-chat. I much prefer our long silences, from six to nine, while
you are working and papa reads. [. . .]

Tell papa that the last conversation we had in the visiting room
made me very happy. I am indeed looking forward to vacation
because then I'll have conversations like that with him every day.

CHARLES

A. E. HOUSMAN *(1859–1936)*

*A. E. Housman, a pagan as a child, then a deist at fifteen, and already a poet
at the age of eight, was once all set, with an umbrella atop a roof, to take up—
or down—parachuting, but was stopped just before he jumped. He lost his
mother on his birthday: she died as he turned twelve. His letters addressed to
"My dear Mamma" are to his mother's bridesmaid, Lucy, whom his father
eventually married. As the eldest child of many, Alfred promised her that he
would help in the raising and enlightening of his siblings, so he became
something of a mother himself. His first famous volume of poems is* A
Shropshire Lad, *which he himself was not. Here he provides a verbal sketch
of John Ruskin, the English author and art and social critic, who was a
popular lecturer as well.*

Thursday [Postmark 29 November 1877]
St John's College

My dear Mamma,

. . . Nothing very remarkable has happened. I go to Ruskin's
lectures, which end on Saturday. I have received the great-coat,
which is very nice . . .

This afternoon Ruskin gave us a great outburst against modern times. He had got a picture of Turner's, framed and glassed, representing Leicester and the Abbey in the distance at sunset, over a river. He read the account of Wolsey's death out of *Henry VIII*. Then he pointed to the picture as representing Leicester when Turner had drawn it. Then he said, 'You, if you like, may go to Leicester to see what it is like now. I never shall. But I can make a pretty good guess.' Then he caught up a paintbrush. 'These stepping-stones of course have been done away with, and are replaced by a be-au-ti-ful iron bridge.' Then he dashed in the iron bridge on the glass of the picture. 'The colour of the stream is supplied on one side by the indigo factory.' Forthwith one side of the stream became indigo. 'On the other side by the soap factory.' Soap dashed in. 'They mix in the middle—like curds,' he said, working them together with a sort of malicious deliberation. 'This field, over which you see the sun setting behind the abbey, is now occupied in a *proper* manner.' Then there went a flame of scarlet across the picture, which developed itself into windows and roofs and red brick, and rushed up into a chimney. 'The atmosphere is supplied —thus!' A puff and cloud of smoke all over Turner's sky: and then the brush thrown down, and Ruskin confronting modern civilisation amidst a tempest of applause, which he always elicits now, as he has this term become immensely popular, his lectures being crowded, whereas of old he used to prophesy to empty benches.

How he confuted the geological survey, and science in general, by the help of the college cook I have no time to tell you, but I remain, with love to father and all, your affectionate son

ALFRED E. HOUSMAN

IVAN TURGENEV *(1818–1883)*

FROM HIS MOTHER, VARVARA PETROVNA TURGENEV

The Russian author of Fathers and Sons *had much more trouble with his mother, Varvara Petrovna, who beat her two sons regularly for the slightest offense or for no reason at all, yet waxed sentimental, possessive, obsessive when Ivan was away. Sending a spy along to keep an eye on him while he was studying in Berlin, she insisted Turgenev tell her every intimate detail of his life, and she wrote him when his letters were not coming often enough:*

I am indulgent enough, it seems to me. But if there are no letters from you in the next post I promise you I shall whip Nikolashka [one of her young servants]. I don't like to do it, he's a very good, nice lad and I am not neglecting him, he is healthy and hard-working. But what can I do? The poor boy will just have to bear it . . . Take care you do not drive me to commit such an injustice.

or me," Varvara Turgenev would say, "everything begins and ends with the two of you. You and your brother. I love you both passionately, but not in the same way. You are the one who hurts me most."

DANTE GABRIEL ROSSETTI (1828–1882)

Rossetti had an extremely pious and proper Victorian mother, whose Biblical knowledge and staunch Catholicism, with its air of mysticism, no doubt influenced the artist's paintings. His themes sprung, often full-blown, from his over-active pre-Raphaelite (and pre-pre-Raphaelite) imagination. Apparently, the Old Testament made a particular impression on Rossetti, for in later years he collected, like Noah, a menagerie of animals (although not necessarily in pairs), in order, he explained, to stanch his flow of morbid thoughts. He kept a raccoon, who happily devoured raw eggs, and a wombat, who frisked about the dinner table after meals when the men sat with brandy and cigars: it died, in fact, of consuming cigars, and Rossetti wrote a poem about it. An unusual son-and-mother pair he owned were two kangaroos, who squabbled continuously and finally killed each other. Peacocks and monkeys roamed freely inside and out, except when squeamish visitors came to call. (A peacock once tangled with a gazelle—and got its tail feathers not only ruffled but smartly flattened.) Rossetti once gave a party to celebrate the awakening of his white dormice from hibernation, according to actress Ellen Terry. "They're awake now," he announced, "but how quiet they are! How full of innocent repose!" He prodded them, and cried, "Wake up!" But the mice were dead.

50 Charlotte Street, Portland Place,
Sunday, 25th June, 1843

My dear Mamma,

'Better late than never,' as the cat said to the kitten when the latter relinquished the Wellington boot in despair. And now, having sent preliminaries to pot in one pithy and well-concocted sentence, I shall proceed forthwith to news.

Yesterday Aunt Margaret, Wiliam, and myself, betook ourselves in the afternoon to 15 Park Village East, having been thereunto invited. The first thing I did on my arrival was to enter the office of Uncle Henry. The air therein was however so suffocating, owing to the press of clients, that I effected a hasty retreat, leaving William to the full enjoyment of the black hole of Calcutta. I then proceeded to the parlour, where I dawdled about till teatime. When I repaid myself by walking into the Coburg with awful perseverance. After tea I went up to Grand-mamma's room where I amused myself with books &c. until it was time to cut. Aunt Eliza wishes me to say that she has had Aunt Charlotte's seal mended and has shelled out therefore and otherwise thereupon expended the sum of one shilling. All these law expressions are attributable solely and entirely to the presence of Uncle Henry who sends you word that your letter came safely to hand, and also that he had received no communication of any sort from the Gloucester boy. I shall tomorrow migrate with the check to Austin Friars; an undiscovered country from whose bourne I fear that I shall not return for some time since I have no idea whatever of its locality.

I finished yesterday the first volume of *Ten Thousand a Year,* the commencement of which, as Aunt Margaret intends to testify in her next epistle, is very unpromising. As it proceeds however it becomes splendid; and, having completed the volume, I laid it down with the impression that it was equal to Dickens. Tomorrow I hope to begin the second volume. William is also perusing *Charles O'Malley,* which he finds very entertaining. [. . .]

I have nearly finished studying the bones, and my next drawing will most probably be an anatomy-figure.

Everybody at 15 Park Village East and at 50 Charlotte Street sends his or her love to everybody at 9 High Street, Hastings. And so, having nothing more to say,

Believe me,
My dear Mamma,
Your affectionate Son,
Gabriel Rossetti

FYODOR DOSTOEVSKY (1821–1881)

Dostoevsky, who in later life went through several political and spiritual persuasions, charted the course of high drama in his novels Notes from Underground, Crime and Punishment, The Brothers Karamazov, *and* The Possessed. *He is already in the grip of a dark melancholy at the age of twelve as he wrote his mother upon first leaving home for boarding school. His overblown prose style is also developing, resounding in the depths of his Russian soul. "The truth is," he said toward the end of his life, "I find it terribly difficult to write letters. I have no talent for it." Yet over nine hundred of them are in print in four volumes. And who knows how many more escaped being captured between book covers, and are running loose in Russia?*

[To Maria Dostoevskaya]
[April–May 1834 Moscow]

Dear Mama,

When you left, dear Mama, I started to miss you terribly, and when I think of you now, dear Mama, I am overcome by such sadness that it's impossible to drive it away, if you only knew how much I would like to see you and I can hardly wait for that joyous moment. Every time I think of you I pray to God for your health. Let us know, dear Mother, whether you arrived safely, kiss Andryushenka and Verochka for me. I kiss your hands and will remain your obedient son.

F. Dostoevsky

E. B. WHITE *(1899–1985)*

Co-creator of Strunk and White's The Elements of Style *and spinner of the childhood favorite* Charlotte's Web, *American writer and humorist Elwyn Brooks White grew up in a household where music, albeit badly played, permeated the atmosphere. His father was the president of a musical instrument and piano company, and would bring home samples—guitars, banjos, ukeleles, cellos—for White and his five siblings to play with cacophonous enthusiasm. "Like my father, I liked the sound of music, but was too lazy to follow it to its source," White confessed. Still, he must have followed it somewhere, as evidenced in the cadence of the following letter written to his mother, Jessica Hart White, from college.*

[Ithaca, N.Y.]
[December 1918]
Wednesday

Dear Ma,

It is time, so I see, for my mid-week's effusion which I'll start with the sad news that, through some delusion, you've been led to believe that our Christmas vacation has entirely escaped from war's grim depredation. The date of my homecoming, if you remember, is Saturday morn—21st of December.

This error corrected, I gracefully turn to the topics of interest, and first you should learn that in spite of the Ithaca weather's contortions (this topic alone might assume large proportions), I now—this is really a subject for prose—am entirely rid of my cold in the nose. My health is restored—I am chipper and brisk, to be brief I'm convinced that it's taking no risk to give to the world—though you never can tell—the astounding report that I'm perfectly well.

This morning came news of my utter redemption from deepest of gloom, for I got an exemption from any more of those weekly abortions which the English Department deals out in large portions—which is merely to say in a casual way, that I don't have to write so much stuff every day.

There's been nothing extraordinary happened of late—there'll be lots more to do when we're able to skate. Just at present the pond is quite infirm of purpose and it wouldn't be I that would step on its surface.

It's time I was leaving to go to the town; through the tortuous graveyard I'll shamble down, twixt tombs to the right of me, tombs to the left of me, tombs in front of me, gaping in silence.

I make this last statement with naught of compunction, that, if in these lines you perceive aught of unction, you must know that this vile deed (I see you are frowning) is due to an over abundance of Browning.

Thanking you lots for the interest money, I beg to remain

Most lovingly

Sonny

GEORGE ELIOT (1819–1880)
TO HER STEPSON CHARLES LEWES

George Eliot's books were her children. "Mrs. Lewes," observed her common-law husband, George Lewes, in reference to her latest novel The Mill on the Floss, *"after a reviving trip [to Florence] will rock the cradle of the new little stranger with fresh maternal vigour." But the author of* Middlemarch *enjoyed a union with Lewes that presented her with three ready-made, oversized, boisterous, real-life teenaged sons. And when they were all home from school at once, she would observe with bewilderment, "We are up to the ears in Boydom." She was closest to Charles, the eldest, who shared her love of music. And she sometimes found it was easier to love him through letters than in the flesh. "Die Mutter," she wrote, "thinks of her dear Boy very much and loves him better than ever now she is at a distance from him."*

Florence, May 27. 61

Dearest Boy,

Jubilate! we shall soon be home again—if indeed you are not learning to do without us so well that our presence will hardly be a matter of jubilation. . . . This evening we have been mounting to the top of Giotto's tower—a very sublime getting-upstairs indeed, and our muscles are much astonished at the unusual exercise; so you must not be shocked if my letter seems to be written with dim faculties, as well as with dim light.

It made me feel hot and tired to read of your being out late three nights running! Nevertheless we have rejoiced at your having pleasant musical evenings [. . .]

Our life has varied little since Pater wrote you his last description. We have seen no one but Mrs. [Thomas] Trollope and her pretty little girl Beatrice, who is a musical genius. She is a delicate fairy about ten years old, but sings with a grace and expression that makes it a thrilling delight to hear her. . . . We have had glorious sunsets shedding crimson and golden lights under the dark bridges across the Arno. All Florence turns out at eventide, but we avoid the slow crowds on the Lung' Arno and take our way "up all manner of streets"—to please a certain wilful pig, of course. You must write to us again, but Pater is going to add his say, and he will give you directions about the address. I have said nothing after all—but here is the pith of all possible letters from me—that I am

Your loving

Mutter.

YOUNG MAN

A Room of One's Own

Nikos Kazantzakis

*I have my books in the suitcases, and my room's like a boat
ready to sail*

e. e. cummings

In short (as Mr. Micawber would say) I am "earning my own living"

Gustave Courbet

My biggest problem is a bed frame and a straw mattress

Paul Klee

*For I know that it is no joke, especially for newcomers, to endure with
good humor all the hocus-pocus of the lordly academes*

Wyndham Lewis

You mustn't think I'm intoxicated, but I really forget how old I am

Vladimir Nabokov

Not having a corner to oneself is simply torture at times

Nikos Kazantzakis (1885–1957)

Like many aspirant young artists and writers, Kazantzakis had his spell in Paris, taking courses in philosophy ("I'm learning the ABCs") and adding his own flavors and colors to the City of Light's joie de vivre. Kazantzakis was radiant and infused with his homeland whatever the circumstances, illuminated by love for his mother and sisters, so present even when far away. Since we'll soon run into another pungent allusion to the last detail of this letter, we'll enlighten you here: Nikos Kazantzakis's mother glazed his linen with tar to ward off sickness — linen we shall whiff again in Florence.

[Paris, no date, but among letters of 1908]

In my room (Anestasia, thank you for not frowning), there's a fire burning all day long. And it's very fine to sit in the warmth, drink your tea and read while it snows outside, and from time to time you open the curtains of the windows and see the world all white. The only bad thing is that my friends like my room too, and there they are often coming up the stairs and ringing the bell . . . for me to open up. I pretend I can't hear, and hold my breath so they'll think I'm out. But they understand and call out to me, "We won't budge from here unless you open up. . . ."

What can I do? I get up and open for them, scolding them as I let them in. They sit on the couch or in the easy chairs, set about lighting the stove by themselves, find the sugar, tea, biscuits, and make tea . . . "Do you want any?" they call to me. Do I want any! And in the big cup, to boot!

And so we drink our tea. Sometimes they have some cognac or champagne outside and we sip away . . . and in this way we waste quite a few evenings! And it pleases my landlady, because, she says, they make me let off a bit of steam after my studying. If you saw her, Mother, you'd kiss her, and make her put some tar in her clothes to keep her strong.

[Paris]
[1909]

Beloved Mother, Anestasia, and Eleni,

. . . Sometimes at night, when I'm reading under my lamp with the green shade, and it's snowing outside and the fire is lit, Mathilda comes in or her sister, Susan, holding their embroidery, and they ask me, "Will you let me keep you company a bit? I'd embroider this band a bit more, but I'm sleepy. Here I don't feel sleepy. So will you let me?" And I raise my head and say to her, "With pleasure. But if you want to oblige me, light the stove and make some tea because I'm not in the mood to . . ." "Ah, avec plaisir."

And all the time the water's boiling and Mathilda or Susan is bending over her embroidery, I keep saying to myself, I'd give half my life to have Anestasia and Eleni sitting here and Mother sitting on the couch facing me, crocheting the tips of her stockings. . . .

I'm terribly upset because it's taken so long to get the money and I have to borrow every day. And worst of all, I have my books in the suitcases, and my room's like a boat ready to sail, just like at home, every time you do the laundry. . . .

e. e. cummings *(1894–1962)*

Cummings sets up housekeeping, scoffs at punctuality, deflects financial assistance, and credits beds with both intellectual and sledlike properties. The "we" here refers to his roommate, painter Arthur "Tex" Wilson, with whom the poet shared digs while he worked for P. F. Collier & Son, mail-order booksellers.

[21 East 15th St., New York]

[January 20, 1917]

Dear Mother

. . . The watch arrived O.K.—I mean, of course, it wasn't running, and hasn't since, but its striker is immensely soothing on rough winter nights. Also the "comforter," tea-service, 2 gray blankets, etc. came duly. And yes, we have bought beds. They are very intellectual, not to say aesthetic; and with the proper treatment will soon become emotional; but not over-emotional, you understand. Also mattresses. The pillows are an improvement, I really think, over my improvisation, which was: To raise the head-end of mattress, insert total no. soiled clothes, and allow said end to fall, producing a parabola, which acted as a tobaggan, spiriting the human body toward the floor. [. . .] I am, by the way, returning the most generous check which accompanied Dad's letter, as (a) We are alright and not really in need of a single thing (in fact, the trouble is to find a reputable burglar to remove our superfluous stuff) and, what is even more important, (b) the "bet" which I consistently refused to make I still and with equal consistency refuse to make—for the very good reason that I have rarely been on time in the past, and expect to be hardly more so in the future; that 1 shoe-shine lasts me a week, and—but I spare your weeping blushes. In short (as Mr. Micawber would say) I am "earning my own living," and as I find it excessively banal, I had rather not mix it up with any more pleasant methods, such as accepting, borrowing (etc.) that which is popularly known as "mazuma" from source or sources other than this dear, beloved, sweet, beneficent, spunky "office," or "<u>firm</u>" as some prefer to name it. [. . .]

GUSTAVE COURBET *(1819–1877)*

Courbet's independence continues to blossom in his quest to acquire a very large room of his own — an artist's studio-cum-living quarters crying out for furniture.

[Paris]
[December 24, 1842]

Dear family:

I have finally found an atelier, at rue de la Harpe, no. 89, and I have rented it. It is the former chapel of the Collège Narbonne, which was made into an atelier for M. Gatti de Gamond, a well-known painter. It is currently used as a music studio by M. Habeneck, the conductor at the Opera. I have rented it for 280 francs a year, or twenty-three francs a month. Now I still have to buy some furniture, including a bed, a chest of drawers, a table, and a bedside table, and some chairs. [. . .] My biggest problem is a bed frame and a straw mattress, but I think that if I look around I will be able to rent, if not buy them. Now you must send me immediately [. . .] two pairs of sheets, a blanket, washcloths and towels, I believe that is all [. . .] Make sure that Liégeon packs those things immediately and does not store them in the rain. And have them delivered to my new lodgings, 89 rue de la Harpe. [. . .]

[. . .] My best wishes for a happy New Year to Grandmother and Grandfather, as well as Mother, Father, sisters, everybody. With a warm embrace,

GUSTAVE

PAUL KLEE (1879–1940)

Swiss painter Paul Klee kept himself free from various art movements and cliques just as he kept himself free, when young, from the academy and its conventions. His painting, with its own ludic philosophical aesthetic, shows his affinity with primitive art and children's art as well as Cubism. With his big, handsome, voracious eyes he studied ideograms, pictograms, cave paintings, and hex signs, sharing with these forms a sense about art as a "language of signs," and for him these signs were also triggers. The following letter from his brief ambivalent submission to art school does not intimate the lyrical imagination and feel for language that are manifest in his diaries and the titles of his paintings, which include The Bavarian Don Giovanni, Viaducts Break Rank, *and* Dance You Monster to My Soft Song!

Munich

October 21, 1898

Dear Mama,

Today I received your letter and Mathilde's card. As soon as I received the latter I went to the Red Rooster and fetched her first card, and then I went, getting lost on the way, to the freight office. There I was told: hasn't come yet. [. . .]

You speak of landscapes, engraving, Lenbach—1) In the winter one cannot do landscapes. 2) To engrave, one must first know how to draw. 3) Lenbach is not the director, but Professor Löffzg. 4) That "absolutely certain" of Herr Homberg sounds absolutely ridiculous. [. . .]

Breakfast costs 30 pfennig. Heat is reckoned according to how you use it. [. . .] I am very content here. Lack for nothing. I enjoy drawing nudes, the more the better.

Send everything I have forgotten. The knife, too, because I'm using a borrowed one. Finally: Lenbach paints landscapes too. The cold only lasted three days. Trip boring as far as Lake Constance. It may be beautiful from Lindau to Munich; I don't know much about it because I slept through that stretch.

From this weird order of answers to your dear letter you can guess how much time I have for writing. Nevertheless I want to try to behave a little more decently. Aside from my disconcerting inexperience in figure drawing (only today my nude figures toppled over), I am nevertheless glad that I did not go to the Academy. For I know that it is no joke, especially for newcomers, to endure with good humor all the hocus-pocus of the lordly academes. [. . .] The drill at the Academy is terrible, they say. So much needless waste of time. And the time is so expensive. These are approximately the views of my colleagues—all very nice, gay fellows. There is one older student in particular who has taken some pains with me, and I have already learned a lot from him. Name? When it comes to drawing nudes most of them are practiced to the point of virtuosity. My comfort is an old fellow with a big mustache who entered today and also daubs away heartily. In drawing heads, on the other hand, they are all still daubers. But such nonsense! The man poses a very young girl, and we're supposed to bring out a likeness! When I said: Why that? "Just because it's hard." That's how things are in the Munich schools. And when I said: "No beginner can do anything with that." "Just wait a couple of years, and you'll find it even harder. By then your naïveté has gone to hell and you fall back on all the well-known tricks of the trade. Then it's a worse mess than ever." Tempting prospect, isn't it?

Well, we will see. If it really turns out to be a matter of staying in the same place, I'll simply go in for landscape next spring. [. . .] N. B.: I still think, with good reason, that there would be no sense attending the university. Greetings. To Herr Leuenberger too. Greetings! Greetings! Greetings!

Paul

I have been writing so much about myself that I've quite forgotten to wish you good health.

WYNDHAM LEWIS *(1884–1957)*

After completing his studies at Slade School of Art, Lewis left London for the Continent. He would live there from 1902 to 1909, spending most of that time in Paris, drawing, painting, and writing, with short sojourns in Munich, Holland, and Madrid. In black cape and with a large black hat, he cut quite the dashing figure in Montparnasse and the Latin Quarter — he fictionalized his romantic persona and experiences in this ambience in his novel Tarr. *Mrs. Lewis's unwavering belief in his talent and her tolerance of the vagaries of his* vie de bohème *(which she helped finance) no doubt invited the candor that characterizes the letters from her prolific, profligate, and gadabout son, who wrote her of his love affairs, aesthetics, ambitions, and breakthroughs as well as about his laundry and his occasional chronological disorientation.*

19 [rue] Mouton–Duvernet [Paris]
[ca. 1904]

Chere Maman.

    You mustn't think I'm intoxicated, but I really forget how old I am, — I couldn't remember yesterday, and it worried me rather: am I 22 years or 23 years old; please let me know by return of post; seriously I actually do forget. —— I'm sorry your cold cant drag itself away from you; but I can quite understand it, — towards the end of the season, the winter, there are so few places for a cold to go to, that when it finds itself well treated it's apt to stop; I'm sure you spoil it, and make much too much fuss with it. Will you write and tell me exactly what I have or have not to do as regards a packet of dirty clothes? Must I declare them dirty? that you would recognise to be a farce, if you saw them: must I count them and leave the number at the office. If I can merely do them up in brown paper, have them weighed, and post them, — then I'll send them. [. . .]

VLADIMIR NABOKOV *(1899–1977)*

Shortly after starting his second year at Cambridge, Nabokov wrote to his mother about the loss of his other mother: Mother Russia, and their estate, Vyra, and their life in St. Petersburg. Eventually, this became the loss of his mother tongue when he switched to English. He wrote his first, sly, and playful novel in that language, The Real Life of Sebastian Knight, *shortly before his departure from Paris to teach in the United States, where he would later write* Lolita, Pale Fire, Pnin, Ada, *and* Transparent Things.

[October 4, 1920]

Mother dear, yesterday I woke up in the middle of the night, and asked someone—I don't know whom—the night, the stars, God: will I really *never return,* is it really all finished, wiped out, destroyed . . . ? In my sleep I saw black, eye-spotted caterpillars on vines of willow herb, then those yellowy-red wooden chairs, with fretwork backs like horses' heads which, remember, stood under the stairway in *our* house (step, step, step and I would stumble, you would laugh . . .)—Mother, we must return, mustn't we, it cannot be that this has all died, turned to dust—such an idea could drive one mad! I would like to describe every little bush, every stalk in our divine park at Vyra—but no one can understand this. . . . How little we valued our paradise . . . —we should have loved it more pointedly, more consciously. . . . People have come into the room, my spirits have suddenly wrinkled up, can't write any more. Not having a corner to oneself is simply torture at times.

GRAND AND OTHER TOURS, WITH GOSSIP

JOSEPH SPENCE

I ought to let you know the progress of my dress and by what degrees I creep into the habit of a gentleman

JACK KEROUAC

Boy, it's been a lot of fun around here. [. . .] I had about ten girlfriends

SARAH BERNHARDT TO HER SON

They invited me to stay with them and hunt the puma

THOMAS MOORE

I have not got my breakfast yet, and as Shakespeare says, 'with veins unfill'd we're apt to pout upon the morning'

VIRGIL THOMSON

The most fun is to look over their shoulders at the letters they write

MARCEL PROUST

Do not show this letter to my angel of a brother

JOSEPH SPENCE (1699–1768)

Although Joseph Spence is a household name to none but his mother, he eminently takes his place here. A scholar of classics and Oxford don, Spence very much wished to study, observe, and learn on the Continent, but on his modest income, such an undertaking was out of the question. His friend, Alexander Pope, acted as liaison and produced a young man, in Spence's words, "of fine parts, of a very polite turn, and extremely good-natured and humane," the nineteen-year-old Lord Middlesex, in need of a chaperon on his well-funded Grand Tour. As Spence wrote to a friend: "Never were the circumstances of any thing more happy than mine at the present. [. . .] I don't go as a tutor or with any charge, only as a companion: so that there's scarce any room for disobliging."

Lyons,
August 10 [July 30], 1731

Dear Mother,

I received your letter yesterday, and this I hope will set out for you tomorrow. [. . .]

The poor nun, whose execution we were at, looked very much like a dying creature. She was extremely pale and had a face that was neither handsome nor agreeable. My acquaintance as yet in the nunneries does not reach far enough to say whether they are generally pretty. I believe for the most part they are not. If there are two daughters in a family and one of them to be a nun, the parents generally choose out the least handsome, because the other will be more fit to scuffle in the world for a husband. What may make people generally think that nuns are pretty may be this. In most of their houses they have needlework and little trinkets to sell, and when strangers come to the grate they always send the prettiest noviciate they have to offer their ware: there she stands like a milliner, and the prettiest milliners, you know, have always the best custom.

I ought to let you know the progress of my dress and by what degrees I creep into the habit of a gentleman. Ever since we have been at Lyons, my hair (which had six weeks' growth on my forehead and temples at Dijon) has been combed back on a light brown natural wig. It did not comply so well with the mode at first, but every day my barber persecutes it with an ounce of pomatum and then plasters it down with half a pound of powder. After the operation I walk out with what passes for a head of hair very well frosted. My coat is a light camlet with silver buttons, a green silk waistcoat sufficiently daubed with silver lace, and I seem upon the brink of having a pair of stockings to it with silver clocks. With all this, I shall look upon myself to be as much a gentleman as that half of the gentlemen in England who are only so from the clothes they wear. [. . .]

Your most dutiful

JACK KEROUAC *(1922–1969)*

Kerouac's mother, Gabrielle, contributed to his cross-country trip, keeping her boy on his westward way, via Western Union. He was writing the chronicle that captured the zeitgeist through the wanderlust of his own Beat Generation and that called to later generations to follow On the Road.

Denver
July 29 '47

Dear Ma—

My friends were all wonderful to me here, feeding me and giving me places to sleep, but now I want to get to San Francisco and make some money. I haven't a cent left and I'll need $25 to take a bus to California from here, because hitch-hiking is impossible across the desert and the mountains. [...]

The easiest way for you to send me the $25.00 is to go to a Western Union office in Brooklyn when you come out of work, and *wire* me the money [...] That way I'll get it fast, and also you won't have to walk all over Ozone Park to find a Western Union office.

Boy, it's been a lot of fun around here. When I get Alan Temko's typewriter tomorrow [...] I'll write and tell you all about it. I had about ten girlfriends; went up to the mountains; saw an opera; ate swell food, venison steak, at Hal's house; the weather is nice—and I'm staying in a swanky apartment with showers and food and everything. But I want to get going so I can make a lot of money sailing in the Pacific and come home in the Fall and finish my book. Gee, and you can't realize how much I miss you, and the house, and writing in my room. [...] Write me a little letter right away.

Love, Jacky XXX

SARAH BERNHARDT *(1844–1923)*
TO HER SON, MAURICE BERNHARDT

French actress Sarah Bernhardt took the theater with her wherever she went, as revealed in her letters on tour. Her account of a trip to South America in letters to her son Maurice paints a canvas as colorful as Candide's picaresque adventures. In a life where adoration was abundant but real, and ordinary love was scarce, Maurice became her anchor, amid sea storms, alligator shoots, and opening nights alike. Onstage playing Hamlet or Medea or at a writing desk on a ship at sea, Bernhardt was never at a loss for self-expression.

On board the Cotopaxi
11 August 1886

My dear, beloved Maurice,

 I just received your telegram announcing your arrival in Paris ... Oh, how far apart we are, my dear son, and how painful it is for me to count the hours that separate us! While your ship sailed toward France, mine carried me farther and farther away from you. ...

 The first two days of the voyage were stormy, but then the sun came out, and we entered the Straits of Magellan easily under our own steam. The captain was all smiles when—boom—one splendid morning, in calm seas, the ship lurched, went over to one side, then, righting itself violently, ran aground. ... Through the porthole I could see a white house within shooting distance, and—almost touching the ship—cattle somewhat frightened by this big machine. Had the sea been rough, I swear on my honor we would have crashed into the house. This habitation belongs to two Englishmen who live quite alone on this strange barren island, with no hills, no trees, with nothing but coarse yellow grass. They came aboard to see who their unexpected visitors were. On learning that Madame, your mother, was one of them, they told me they had made a four-day trip to Montevideo just to see me perform. They invited me to stay with them and hunt the puma one could see on the low sand dunes in the distance, but the captain begged me not to disembark. I stayed on board, not without regrets. We played baccarat all day, and I won a thousand francs which I deducted from what you owe Grau. I shot at seagulls with Garnier's Winchester, but only managed to damage a buoy. At four o'clock a large German ship appeared on the horizon. It stopped a mile away. Then the German captain came up to us in a launch. . . . Our Captain Hayes seemed very nervous. He took me aside and said: "The German commandant has offered to tow us out to sea, but it's possible he won't succeed. What do you think? Are you afraid of being stranded, or do you have confidence in me?"

"Ah, captain," I said. "I beg you to send him away. I have confidence in you, and in my lucky star," and I touched the good-luck medal you gave me, the one I wear on a chain around my neck. The captain, visibly moved, uttered his open-hearted thanks. That evening at dinner, we drank to his health, and to the tides on which our fate depends. The next day, after hours of hard labor on the part of the engine and the crew, the vessel righted itself, and we cast off. There my darling, you have the story of my little odyssey.

12 August 1886

. . . This morning I take up the story of our voyage. The Straits of Magellan provided a superb spectacle: a chain of mountains covered with vegetation and snow. [. . .] Ah! How I thought of you, my dear little Maurice, especially when some Patagonians came up to us. They stopped their pirogue at the foot of our ship. There were three men and four women, one with a small infant on her back. The women had red skin and shaved heads with a tuft of thick, black hair. Their wide bony faces were smiling and full of charm. They wore cloaks of guanaco or sealskin. One man was nude to the waist with breeches of fine black cloth; another wore a short, checked English jacket. Yet another had on women's stockings, a pair of chestnut-colored men's underpants cut above the knee, and a flannel waistcoat. The women asked for biscuits in their sweet voices, saying "Gayetta! Gayetta!" They also liked to repeat an English phrase which throws the entire crew into wild fits of laughter. No one would translate it for me, as it was taught them by sailors and is very naughty. [. . .]

At last we resumed our voyage. [. . .] Our arrival at Cape Silas was horrible: four days and nights fighting a raging wind. The noise was infernal; the whole ship creaked; and everyone clung to the walls.

We sighted Lota at four in the morning, five days late. A launch covered with flowers was sent out to meet us. As soon as I set foot in it, music was heard: *La Marseillaise* followed by the national anthem of Chile.

[. . .] When we arrived, a motley crowd of miners, both women and men, were waiting for us. The two-hundred-foot descent into the underground is very dramatic, much like the descriptions in Zola's *Germinal*. Once in the mine, I was overcome with emotion. The miners were lined up in their shabby work-clothes, lamps attached to their foreheads. One of them presented me with palm fronds. Sweet, plaintive music could be heard. It was so poignant that we all began to weep. Oh, that beautiful day in which nothing was lacking except your sweet presence. But I feel that way every time something gives me pleasure. I hope you do not have the same sadness. . . .

Thomas Moore *(1779–1852)*

Diminutive, curly-haired, and with an upturned nose set in a perennially upturned face (all the better to converse with his taller chums), Irish poet Thomas Moore delighted in a stage-door mom who never had to leave home. As an infant, he was nourished on a steady diet of robust musical soirees in Anastasia Moore's Dublin parlor. At five, he joined the players by reciting Hamlet's soliloquies (his quotes in this letter come from Shakespeare, by the way). So solicitous of his studies was Anastasia that when she would come home late from a musical night out, she'd wake her son and have him read his lessons, no matter the time. He'd bounce up from sleep like an India-rubber ball, and happily start reciting on the spot. Also a gifted songbird, Moore later composed song lyrics and poems while in perpetual motion, and he scarcely sat down at parties as an adult, although one acquaintance metaphorically recalled his "cat-like disposition to curl himself up near something or somebody comfortable." He did sit still long enough to write Anastasia faithfully, including news of his early London success, Odes of Anacreon. *He sent the first copy to his mother, and knowing already that she would praise him, exulted greedily, "How did you look at it? What did you feel? Oh! I know what you felt, and I know how you looked!" Here he revels in descriptions of English society members with whom he rubbed elbows.*

Nov. 14. 1799.
[writing from Manchester]

Dear Mama,

I have left now so many days of this week without writing, that my letters will come 'not single *spies,* but in *battalions.*'

Beresford Burston and I will dine together to-morrow or the next day, I believe. He appears to me to be drinking deep the intoxications of this place. I was out very late last night at a party at the Honourable Mrs. Gardiner's. She is an *English* woman, but has an *Irish heart*. On Sunday last you know I was to dine at Incledon's. Johnson and I got very great: he is to introduce me to Colman, the manager and author. I met there too Dr. Mosely, the king's physician. He took my address, and seemed to wish the cultivation of an acquaintance: he is in the first circles. Poor Incledon is deplorably hoarse: we might say to him, what he himself said to Peter Duffey (coal factor) the first time he heard him sing, 'By the holy St. Peter, you hav'nt a *note* in your *sack*.' Miss Biggs, the present heroine of Drury Lane, dined there, and gave me her orders for the ensuing evening. Lord Moira is in town. I left my card with him yesterday. I am very much afraid that you did not get my letter with the inclosure for Cuming; let me know immediately. I have not got my breakfast yet, and as Shakespeare says, 'with veins unfill'd we're apt to *pout* upon the morning.' Has the music-book been procured from Mrs. Grierson's for Dr. S? I hope it has. Farewell, my good mother. Believe me, with the tenderest remembrances to my father and my dear little girls, yours ever.

VIRGIL THOMSON (*1896–1989*)

Musician, critic, composer, and champion of modernism in all forms, Virgil Thomson was proud of his Kansas City roots, even though his career took off in New York and Paris. His first food for thought was served up at his mother's dining room table. She would hold Sunday suppers, where sixteen-year-old Thomson was encouraged to invite a wide circle of friends of all ages involved in music and the arts. He later explained that here he had hoped "to create and sustain a symposium of the arts." These Sunday nights were perfect training for the salons of Paris he would later participate in and even preside over, not unlike Gertrude Stein, with whom he collaborated to create the opera Four Saints in Three Acts. *A far cry, however, from the sophistication of salons was military camp during World War I, which Thomson sketches in detail in a letter to his mother, almost as if he were describing the setting for an opera or a play.*

[To Clara May Gaines Thomson]
Tuesday night, October 23, 1917

My dear mother:

. . . I enjoy coming to the Y to write letters. In the first place, I can think better than I can with the fellows in the tent talking around me and at me and over me. And then, it is a variety, a change of scene that refreshes my mind when I haven't left the company street all day. And I can sit and watch the fellows write. The seats at the long writing tables soon fill up, and the others who want to write have to find themselves a corner. Some sit on one seat and write on the seat in front, for the long benches have no backs; some kneel on the floor, putting the paper on the seat. Sometimes they put one bench on another for a desk, while a benchful of soldiers lines up on each side of this. Some kneel around the platform. Some go back to their tents.

The attitudes they take are especially curious too. One will sprawl his elbows out on the desk and let his pencil flow swiftly, while another will cramp himself up and write by wriggling his fingers. And the left-handed ones write almost upside down.

The most fun is to look over their shoulders at the letters they write. A chap will begin vigorously, "My dearest darling Louise," and then stop. Pretty soon he will get a thought and go ahead. "Although we have only met once, I again must assure you that I love you dearly and that you are the only girl I write to." And so on. The next letter comes easier, because he has already thought this up, and so he writes it over again to the girl he met at some Kansas town on the way down. The man next to him may be assuring his mother that the food is good and that he is happy, and the fellow just across will be telling how hard he is worked and how unfairly treated and how bum the victuals and scarce and how vile and insufferable the weather. I suppose they are all sincere, whether they ramble on or not; and there are grounds for any manner in which the different men are affected. But those who complain would probably complain no matter where they were.

The little cakes were fine, a great hit. There were enough for two messes after supper. How on earth did you ever make them? Were they iced separately? The jelly was good, although we argued about the flavor.

I had a new experience yesterday as K.P. (meaning kitchen police). I did a little of everything. I peeled onions and potatoes. I washed pots. I drew water. I piled cord wood in a dust storm. I ran the coffee urn at meals. I emptied garbage. I sprinkled the floor and swept the tables. I nearly sawed wood.

Tell sister to write again. Her other letter was fine.

With love,
Virgil

Marcel Proust (1871–1922)

Barely do those tisaned crumbs of madeleine transport Marcel Proust into a tempo unparalleled now or then, than he has us at his bedside, where he wishes his maman would arrive and remain. While most of Remembrances of Things Past *is concerned with other characters cast from the past, in life Proust and his mother kept a close watch on each other, sharing* inquiétudes, *asthma and other sufferings, his development as a writer, and gossip in their own private code: amused, ironic, with pointed observations and veritable swells, at times, of nuance. Throughout the writing of his masterpiece, Proust tucked himself into bed after the crack of dawn.*

Dear reader, do not have a fit of neurasthenia or asthma yourself if the Compte d'Eu, M. Joubert, and the charming Duchesses here are strangers to you. Just pretend they're characters captured in Remembrances of Things Past, *where they no doubt* do *appear among composites assembled by Proust out of the society in which he climbed, through which he glided, wrapped in muffler and greatcoat.*

Thursday, half-past one

[Evian, probably September 24, 1899]

Ma chère petite Maman,

The "Eu" appear to be nice simple people, although I make a point of keeping on my hat and standing aloof in a "not-on-speaking-terms-since-Rennes" attitude. Having found myself in front of a door with the old man, and one of us having to go through first, I drew aside. And he passed me, taking off his hat with a deep bow, not at all condescending or d'Haussonville, but just the bow of a very polite, good old man, the kind I have not yet had from any of the persons from whom I draw aside in the same way, "simple bourgeois," who pass by as stiff as kings. And speaking of kings, Comte d'Eu, instead of walking, glides over the floor as though he were on skates. But I dare not conclude *à la Cuvier* that this is merely good manners, not knowing whether this gliding motion is due to his gout or to memories of the Court. Do not show this letter to my angel of a brother, who is an angel but also a judge, a severe judge who might see in my remarks about Comte d'Eu a snobbishness or a frivolity very remote from my real feelings, rather than my need of telling you what we would love to talk about, and the kinds of remarks that amuse us.

M. Joubert, having made the mistake of accepting the office of Inspector from his friend, Fontanes, Regent of the University, managed to ruin his very frail health. He had to stay in bed the better part of each day. "But his friends, deprived of his visits, were unwilling to give up the charms of his conversation, and his bed was regularly surrounded by the cleverest wits and the most charming women. M. de Chateaubriand and the Duchesses de Duras and de Lévis were most punctilious about coming to enjoy his conversation." I hope we are close enough in spirit for you not to think I mean to infer that one should stay in bed, etc., etc. I am copying this with a smile, *cum grano salis,* because of the analogy, except for the part about the duchesses. . . .

Mille tendres baisers,
Marcel

Linen, Clothes,
Evasions of
Marriage, Elopements

Gustave Courbet

I am sending you my dirty laundry

Gustav Mahler's mother

Are you going to end up changing your lodgings every time you change your linen?

Henri de Toulouse-Lautrec

I haven't the energy to go to the shirt-maker's

Gustave Flaubert

When I look at myself in the mirror, it seems to me that I should have trouble turning around

Anthony Trollope

but this also we must discuss on a gondola

Wyndham Lewis

henceforth I will no more implant kisses on her blanched brow or stroke her bosom

Percy Bysshe Shelley

send me the Galvanic Machine & Solar Microscope

GUSTAVE COURBET (1819–1877)

Courbet, self-proclaimed leader of the French Realist school of painting, addresses the realities of his everyday life and clamors for cotton socks, no small partiality in the world of comfort. Socks, songs—ah, but surely it was the illustrations that sang, tucked into this parcel.

[Besançon]
[April (?) 1839]

Dear family:

I am sending you my dirty laundry. [. . .] I am sending you my woollen socks because I don't wear them. Send me cotton socks. I am also sending you the songs, and two small prospectuses of a little book by a friend of mine for which, to oblige him, I have done some illustrations.

Gustave Courbet

GUSTAV MAHLER *(1860–1911)*
FROM HIS MOTHER, MARIE MAHLER

It sounds like Marie Mahler (who would have been in heaven with a cellular phone) kept tugging her son Gustav back down to the realities of house-keeping when the Austrian composer, here a youth of twenty-two, would rather have been soaring with his muse in the firmament. One can picture him wrapped in a towel, discarded trousers and shirts cascading behind him as he rises, dancing, to celestial heights, accompanied by his muscle-bound symphonies laced with Jewish folk tunes—thumping down long enough, of course, to compose The Song of the Earth.

Iglau
15 December 1882

Dear Gustav,

. . . Will you write now to let us know if you are coming? and when? so that I can warm your room. I shall also be able to argue out with you those things I can't argue out in letters. Why these endless changes of lodgings? I don't believe there can be a single person apart from you who changes his lodgings every fortnight. Are you going to end up changing your lodgings every time you change your linen? [. . .] And won't you finally find yourself without any linen or clothes? I know you: you will forget something at each place—and will go on moving until you have nothing left. Am I not right? However I shall leave the rest until I can talk to you. That is enough for today. One more thing, though: if you come home bring with you a bottle of *French brandy.*

Good-bye and warmest regards from us all,

Your ever-loving Mother,
Marie

Henri de Toulouse-Lautrec *(1864–1901)*

[Paris, November 1884]

[. . .] I'm back in the old routine that will last until spring and then maybe I'll do some really bizarre things. All vague yet.

I haven't had the energy to go to the shirt-maker's. Too pooped even to think of going out. It's so nice in the evenings at Grenier's in the warm studio. It would be nice if you were to knit me a stocking cap and slippers. The cafés bore me, going downstairs is a nuisance, painting and sleeping, that's all there is.

I'll stop because I'm getting mumbly-wumbly.

And a kiss for the grandmas, aunts, and you.

Yours,

HTL

[Paris]

9 August [1892]

My dear Mama,

You are definitely the hen who hatched a famous duck. I was amused this morning, while I was with Papa in the carriage, to take a flop in the place de la Madeleine without suffering a scratch, except for my pince-nez, which put my nose a little out of joint. I had a doctor friend check me out, and he found *nothing*. So I'm leaving tomorrow for Bordeaux, and I'll have lunch on Thursday at Soulac.

I'll write to you.

Yours,

Henri

I'm writing you this letter to spare you the gossip in the newspapers.

GUSTAVE FLAUBERT *(1821–1880)*

The author of Madame Bovary *and* A Sentimental Education *gave a swift and unbridled reply when his mother, Madame Flaubert, wrote to Gustave that she would meet him in Italy, and, in the same letter, informed him of the marriage of his friend Ernest Chevalier. She more than hinted that it was time he too settle down with a wife, have a family: after all, he was twenty-nine.*

When is the wedding to be, you ask me, apropos of the news of Ernest Chevalier's marriage. When? Never, I hope. As far as a man can answer for what he will do, I reply in the negative. Contact with the world—and I've been rubbing shoulders with it now for fourteen months—makes me feel more and more like returning to my shell. . . . Besides, if I had to say how I feel deep down, and if it didn't sound too presumptuous, I would say: 'Too late, now. I'm too old to change.' When one has lived, as I have, a completely inner life, full of turbulent analyses and repressed enthusiasms, when one has so frequently excited and calmed oneself by turns, and employed all one's youth in learning to manage one's soul, as a horseman manages his horse . . . well, what I mean is, if one hasn't broken one's neck at the outset, chances are one won't break it later. I, too, am 'established,' in that I have found my seat, my center of gravity. . . . For me, marriage would be an apostasy: the very thought terrifies me. . . . Good old Ernest! There he is, married, established—and a magistrate to boot. What a perfect bourgeois and gentleman! How much more than ever he'll be the defender of order, family, property! But then he has followed the normal course. He too was an artist. [. . .] As a magistrate, he is reactionary; married, he'll be a cuckold; and so, spending his life between his female and his children on the one hand, and turpitudes of his profession on the other, there he will be, the perfect example of the man who has managed to attain everything life has to offer. Phew! Let's talk about something else.

*A*s the reunion of mother and son drew nearer, Gustave alerted her to changes she would notice immediately, although he promised to shave off his beard upon reaching Naples: "Two years from now I shall be completely bald. . . . You will find me if not taller, at least fatter. When I look at myself in the mirror, it seems to me that I should have trouble turning around."

ANTHONY TROLLOPE *(1815–1882)*

Anthony Trollope's mother, Fanny, was a writer of note, as was her son, during England's industrious Victorian era. A longtime employee of the British postal service, Trollope not only created such novels as Barchester Towers *and* Phineas Finn; *he also invented the red iron-pillar box, the English equivalent of the American mailbox and perhaps its forerunner. He even traveled as far as America—where Fanny coincidentally researched her first successful book,* Domestic Manners of the Americans—*in the services of the post office. Here the newly married Anthony vows to defer to his mother's taste not in domestic manners, but in domestic furnishings.*

...Then comes the important question of residence—Where shall we live? We both dislike the north—& the districts may all be changed—but this also we must discuss on a gondola. We wont buy our furniture at any rate till we have discussed with you the colour of the drawing room curtains—

—A.T.

WYNDHAM LEWIS (1884–1957)

When, during a brief stay in Holland, Wyndham Lewis's attentions to his landlord's daughter provoked marital schemes in the bosom of her family, Lewis was quick to lay out the complications to his mother and request her instant complicity in extricating himself from this bourgeois nightmare—not at all the world to sustain the explorations of life and art that were his perpetual purpose.

[Postmarked "Haarlem, 7 Oct. 1904."]
send letters to Poste Restante.

Chere Maman.

Next Wednesday or Thursday my month's up here, and home I come: I have given up copying Hals, and that was the only thing to keep me here: I've done lots of work; and if I can get in 2 or 3 weeks work before the "New English" in London I shall be very glad.

There is alas, a definite reason for my returning: there is a girl here, the daughter of the house, that is very attractive: she's very stupid, uninteresting and not in the least exciting for me; but being exiled from the "fair," I have taken certain opportunities to bestow a kiss upon her blanched brow, and may perhaps have stroked her bosom; but of course I have done nothing more and didn't intend to, as there are too many difficulties and objections in such a case: Well, the mama and papa seem to have noticed these mild attentions.—As I told you not to send my letters here you can imagine that I didn't put very much trust in my hostess: the old man, as far as that goes, is very entertaining, but I don't expect he's much better than the woman. Well, lately, papa has asked a great many questions about you, (I had mentioned the fact that I had a mother,) and Mama informed me a week ago that "of course the furniture would go to her dear daughter Lesbie," at which I scream with laughter, for its the sort of remark Mama's make in Dickens' books, but I thought were too sophisticated to do so in actual life. Papa also, when he's posing for me, talks about marriage etc., also I hear the family having loud disputes very often (one an hour ago; and when I enquired jestingly, was told casually that the subject was marriage-contracts etc.) I think that I am often the subject of these disputes:—also, which is very unpleasant, the people here talk about me in a disagreeable way in the next room, and so on. Now, no power on earth can force you to marry; and I'm sure no power would force me: but people might say you'd trifled with their daughter, and make things unpleasant: henceforth I will no more implant kisses on her blanched brow or stroke her bosom—no: but I had better leave on Wednesday, I think: an air of conspiracy in a house is one of the most unpleasant things imaginable, if you are the object of it.

If you will send me a letter here on monday, *with nothing much inside,* I will say to the people that I had heard something from home, and had better go back to London on Wednesday: giving them still to understand, more or less as I already have done, that it is quite unlikely I will return later, in a month or so: I don't want them to think I'm going for any reason to be found "en famille" [?] here, or they might become unpleasant.—You might write another letter to Poste Restante telling me what you think. I really have a most absurd dread of the very thought of marriage: I feel like packing up and flying to the British Consul for protection.

There is of course no cause whatever for alarm; but when unpleasantness sets in, like the winter winds, I, the swallow, flee away. [. . .]

As it is they ask constantly why you don't write to me, and I cant exactly say I get letters at Poste Restante. . . .

Well, it's nothing to get excited about; but one cant be too careful in these things.

Write immediately . . .

au revoir

I am yours ever

P. W. LEWIS

PERCY BYSSHE SHELLEY *(1792–1822)*

The quintessential English Romantic poet Percy Bysshe Shelley, having eloped, writes his mother in search of forgiveness and his Galvanic Machine. Of Shelley's mother, André Maurois writes in Ariel: The Life of Shelley: *"As to Mrs. Shelley, she had been the prettiest girl in the county, she liked a man to be a fighter, and she would watch with disgust her eldest son go off into the woods carrying a book under his arm instead of a gun."*

St. James's Coffee House

November 7 [for 6] [1812]

My dear Mother,

I write to request you, if you can, to manage to send me the Galvanic Machine & Solar Microscope which I left at Field Place. The latter instrument being essential to a branch of philosophy which I am now pursuing.

I take this opportunity of sending my love to yourself & my sisters, of assuring you that anything I can do for you, in town I will, & that having been rendered by a most disinterested friend to a certain degree <u>independent</u>, my means of serving you in any little matters are by no means so limited as you may suppose.

However you may have felt piqued at the deception which I practised on my marriage, I know you will be glad to hear that I am <u>now</u> one of the happiest of men, & that nothing but the idea of this <u>temporary</u> estrangement from my family prevents me from becoming the happiest.

My dear Mother
Very sincerely your Affectionate Son
Percy B Shelley

The fascination with science started early. At Eton, enveloped by the bluish flames of alcohol in the middle of a circle, Shelley uttered incantations to various elemental demons. "Please, sir, I'm raising the devil," was his reply on another occasion when his master demanded to know what on earth he was doing. The machines he requests of his mother were not his first: as a young boy he had mesmerized his adoring sisters and girl cousins with various demonstrations and electric shocks—except for his littlest sister, Helen, who'd burst into tears the minute he appeared with a bottle and a bit of wire.

This elopement was with his sweet, frivolous child-bride Harriet, not Shelley's second wife, Mary, creator of *Frankenstein*.

THE ARTS, ACCOMPLISHMENTS, AND PRAISE

VLADIMIR NABOKOV

No problem if the poems get lost (I know them by heart anyway)

ROBERT LOUIS STEVENSON

I wish that life was an opera. I should like to live in one. . .

EZRA POUND

Epstein is a great sculptor. I wish he would wash, but I believe Michael Angelo never did, so I suppose it is part of the tradition

MARCEL PROUST'S MOTHER

I gave Watteau regards from you and Hahn, then I cast myself at the feet of Leonardo and Titian (and so many others!!!)

WILLIAM RANDOLPH HEARST

My artistic longings are not altogether distinct from avarice, I am afraid

H. G. WELLS

love to Little Clock Man and Little Daddy and Little Mother

CHARLES BAUDELAIRE

I think you'll be pleased to hear some fine things said about me. It doesn't happen often

JEAN COCTEAU

One of your sons folds his wings / And the other feels his grow again

OSCAR WILDE'S MOTHER

Well, after all, we have genius

THOMAS MOORE

I am happy, careless, comical, everything I could wish

IVAN TURGENEV'S MOTHER

your tale, your poem, smells of wild strawberries

VLADIMIR NABOKOV *(1899–1977)*

Nabokov's mother, Elena, encouraged her son to hoard any gift of the moment, as its value would increase with the years, a gift that would illuminate every story and novel the Russian author would write in either his native or adopted tongue. As Nabokov recounts in Speak, Memory:

"'Vot zapomni [now remember],' she would say in conspiratorial tones as she drew my attention to this or that loved thing in Vyra— . . . the palette of maple leaves on brown sand, a small bird's cuneate footprints on new snow. . . . Thus, in a way, I inherited an exquisite simulacrum—the beauty of intangible property, unreal estate—and this proved a splendid training for the endurance of later losses."

19.vi.23
Soliès-Pont, Alpes Maritimes

My dearest,

Today I received your dear card in which you say you only got two poems (*"Cherries"* and another one), while, *before* them, I had sent you a long letter with the two poems *"Vecher"* and *"Kresti."* No problem if the poems get lost (I know them by heart anyway) but I'm sorry about the letter. . . . Now I send you two short poems (to be followed tomorrow by much better ones) and a longer one (about an actual occurrence; the song *en question* was the romance "Within your eyes, within your wild caress-es . . .").

It is evening now, with touching cloudlets in the sky. I took a walk around the plantation, behind the grove of cork oaks, ate peaches and apricots, admired the sunset, listened to a nightingale's twees and whistles, and both its song and the sunset tasted of apricot and peach.

In a large cage near the house, live, all together (and rather messily), chickens, roosters, ducks, peahens, and white rabbits. One of the rabbits was lying with its front paws extended, like a lop-eared sphynx. Then a chick climbed on its back, and both of them had a scare. . . .

All during these days I have felt drawn to the inkwell, but there's no time for writing. For that reason—and because, without you, the sun is not the same, am coming back no later than July 20. I have gained weight and gotten all dark, since I now wear nothing but shorts when I work. . .

ROBERT LOUIS STEVENSON (1850–1894)

Although Scottish novelist Robert Louis Stevenson of Treasure Island *fame wrote dramatic adventure stories full of hardships, he couldn't sit through an opera fraught with death and destruction without getting weak in the knees— in fact, he didn't, and wrote to Mother instead over a comforting Schnitt while staying in Frankfurt during his student days.*

[To Mrs. Thomas Stevenson]
[13 Rosengasse, Frankfurt]
Tuesday morning, August, 1872.
. . . Last night I was at the theatre and heard *Die Judin (La Juive)*, and was thereby terribly excited. At last, in the middle of the fifth act, which was perfectly beastly, I had to slope. I could stand even seeing the cauldron with the sham fire beneath, and the two hateful executioners in red; but when at last the girl's courage breaks down, and, grasping her father's arm, she cries out—O so shudderfully!— I thought it high time to be out of that *galère,* and so I do not know

yet whether it ends well or ill; but if I ever afterwards find that they do carry things to the extremity, I shall think more meanly of my species. It was raining and cold outside, so I went into a *Bierhalle,* and sat and brooded over a *Schnitt* (half-glass) for nearly an hour. An opera is far more *real* than real life to me. It seems as if stage illusion, and particularly this hardest to swallow and most conventional illusion of them all—an opera—would never stale upon me. I wish that life was an opera. I should like to *live* in one; but I don't know in what quarter of the globe I shall find a society so constituted. Besides, it would soon pall: imagine asking for three-kreuzer cigars in recitative, or giving the washerwoman the inventory of your dirty clothes in a sustained and *flourishous* aria. [. . .]

EZRA POUND (1885–1972)

Ezra Pound, a key image-maker among the Imagist poets in London, wrote grouchier letters to his mother than this one, especially in response to her offers of career or moral guidance. It's refreshing to see that in letters home he was his usual cocky and cantankerous self. Pound was right there with Wyndham Lewis, launching Vorticism with BLAST and defining the innovations of Modernist poetry. As Pound said, "Make it new." He also said "Condensare," so he would not approve a lengthy introduction to this letter about undershirts, Yeats, and unwashed sculptors.

London

November [1913]

Dear Mother: I plan to spend my birthday largesse in the purchase of four luxurious undershirts. Or rather I had planned to do; if, however, the bloody guardsman who borrowed my luxurious hat from the Cabaret cloak room (<u>not</u> by accident) does not return the same, I shall probably divert certain shekels from the yeager. . . .

My stay in Stone Cottage will not be in the least profitable. I detest the country. Yeats will amuse me part of the time and bore me to death with psychical research the rest. I regard the visit as a duty to posterity. . . .

I seem to spend most of my time attending to other people's affairs, weaning young poetettes from obscurity into the glowing pages of divers rotten publications, etc. . . . Conducting a literary kindergarten for the aspiring, etc. etc. . . .

Epstein is a great sculptor. I wish he would wash, but I believe Michel Angelo <u>never</u> did, so I suppose it is part of the tradition. Also it is nearly impossible to appear clean in London, perhaps he does remove some of the grime. . . .

If I am to get anything done this day, I must be off and at it.

Love to you and dad.

MARCEL PROUST *(1871–1922)*

FROM HIS MOTHER, JEANNE PROUST

Revealing a gift for observation and innuendo, Madame Proust sketches an animated picture of the Louvre, filled with fin-de-siècle *painters copying the classics and English tourists momentarily slicing through the silence—and finding themselves the object of her keen* aperçu.

Sunday [25 August 1895?]

My darling,

It's your letters that are sweet, your idea of hugging me unstarched made me burst out laughing.

At the Louvre? I gave Watteau regards from you and Hahn, then I cast myself at the feet of Leonardo and Titian (and so many others!!!). At this season and in the morning the rooms are almost deserted. The occupants are mostly poor wrecks, old women in spectacles, who, though perched on top of ladders to be as close as possible to their models, don't succeed in stealing their celestial fire.

And among the public a few English ladies, whose main concern it is to keep abreast of their catalogues.

Suddenly the calm was shattered by a thundering voice and an uninterrupted flow of words.

Alarmed, I see a group of English ladies and gentlemen emerging, all with binoculars slung over their shoulders (the straps of which strangely divide the airy shirtwaists of the ladies into eastern and western hemispheres), following in the footsteps of a guide, who leads them at a furious pace, stunning them with the names of persons and gods of whom, as poor Louise used to say, 'Old as I am, I can safely say I have never heard of such a thing in all my life'. Listening ecstatically, they kept on running for fear of losing him. As they were leaving the *salon carré* and entering the *grande galerie,* the man negligently thrust out his middle finger behind him and

said without turning round: 'This, *Charles the First,* by Van Dyck.'
Since the tone said: a minor work, they hardly looked. 'Kings of
England,' they said. 'Oh, we've got them at home.' And they hurried
on to catch their guide, who had already entered the next gallery.

WILLIAM RANDOLPH HEARST *(1863–1951)*

*William Randolph Hearst, American media mogul and creator of Hearst's
Castle, and adored son of the formidable Phoebe Hearst, traveled extensively
and often with his mother to Europe throughout his childhood. At a very
young age he was already lusting after a palace of his own, deciding on the
Louvre, which he asked Phoebe to buy for him. He was endlessly curious and
precociously enthralled with art and architecture. When in Europe alone as a
young man, the future voracious collector exposes his growing ardor and advises
Phoebe how to cultivate her own. The selectivity he counsels did not
remain a principle with him, though. At the peak of his wealth and
acquisitiveness, Hearst represented 25 percent of the world's art market, and
what he didn't have room for in his various homes was stored in warehouses in
San Simeon, San Francisco, and New York.*

[January, 1889]
. . . I have the art fever terribly. Queer, isn't it? I never thought
I would get it this way. I never miss a gallery now and I go and
mosey about the pictures and statuary and admire them and wish
they were mine. My artistic longings are not altogether distinct
from avarice, I am afraid. . . .

So I want to have some of these fine things and I want you to
have some of these fine things and do you know, my beloved
mother, there is a way in which you might get them. If, instead of

buying a half a dozen fairly nice things, you would wait and buy one fine thing, all would be well.

As it is at present we have things scattered from New York to Washington . . . to San Francisco, more than a house could hold and yet now among them a half a dozen things that are really superb. . . .

Ansiglioni says it is a great time to buy. The people [of Italy] are heavily taxed; the government is nearly bankrupt and cannot buy up these opportunities [from palaces] itself as it has formerly done, and some wealthy American or Englishman will soon step in and, taking these chances here and there, will have a collection almost equal to that of some of these national galleries.

I wish I could be the rich American. I wish you could be. How nice it would be if we could exchange all our alleged pictures for two or three masterpieces such as I have mentioned. In price, they are the same but in value, how different.

. . . I am not going to buy any more trinkets. . . . Then when advanced in years I will not have had all that I wanted, but I will have all that I want—which is better. Go thou and do likewise, Mama, dear. If you don't, you will be mad at yourself next time you come abroad. What's the good of more trinkets when we haven't room for those we have? Save your money, Momey, and <u>wait</u>. . . .

I see that some Royal Duke of Spain has gone to America with a fine collection of old masters and will sell them there. Get <u>one</u>. Get a Murillo or a Velasquez. Don't get four or five old masters that nobody ever heard anything about. Get a Murillo or a Velasquez. Of course, get a Murillo <u>and</u> a Velasquez if you can but get at least one good picture and wait again.

Your wise and reverent son,
W.R.H.

H. G. Wells (1866–1946)

This English novelist, historian, and social revolutionary penned some of the first science fiction classics, such as The War of the Worlds *and* The Time Machine. *His mother wanted him to be a draper's apprentice, but he rebelled, devouring books and embracing academia, with his own fresh, innovative approach to learning. In this letter, a sense of abundance prevails, amid a flurry of ambitious projects, and Wells dashed off affectionate, funny sketches of his parents and the mysterious Little Clock Man—perhaps one of his early sci-fi creations.*

12, Mornington Road, N.W.

5/12/94

My dear little Mother,

I'm anticipating Christmas and sending you a little present (I wish it could be larger). I'm keeping very well this Christmas and at about the same level of prosperity. I don't do so much for the *P.M.G.* but I do stuff for the *Saturday* which is rather better pay and I have some hope of the *New Review.* . . .

This day week I'm giving my lecture at the Coll of Preceptors. There's nothing settled about any of my books yet but I think there will be two if not three in March.

Let me hear all about you. Have you heard from Fred?

Yours ever affectionately

Bertie.

[*Little Bertie writing away for dear Life to get little things for all his little People sends his love to Little Clock Man & Little Daddy & Little Mother.*]

CHARLES BAUDELAIRE (1821 – 1867)

What a handful is this dandy! His letters to his mother chart a tempestuous course, with the greatest of extremes in his feelings, which seem to rise and fall with his own fortunes and accomplishments, and moods of uncertain provenance, although the spleen is a likely suspect. As critic and translator, Baudelaire would later take under his literary wing America's most tortured motherless child, Edgar Allan Poe—bringing the gothic orphan more blazing fame and acclaim in Europe than he enjoyed during his lifetime in his own country.

Friday, June 6, 1856

My dearest mother, I am now forced to break the rule you imposed on me and that I have imposed on myself: perhaps you don't know that although I am forced to keep my apartment at Rue d'Angoulême for another season, I am no longer living there. I'll have a real address Monday or Tuesday at the latest. They have just reprinted 3000 copies of my little book. This will put some money in my hands and, to give myself the rest I need, I am going to pay all my monthly expenses *in advance*. [. . .]

I would like you to watch for a long article about me in *Le Pays* next Wednesday or Tuesday [. . .] by a very distinguished writer. I think you'll be pleased to hear some fine things said about me. It doesn't happen often.

But this is not all. There are many things you can guess without my telling you. My heart is heavy, heavy with a thousand things. This is the fourth time that I beg you to let me see you again. I don't understand why you refuse so obstinately. I ask you this without offering explanations, I ask it as a tired, wounded man asking for a favor, a tonic, a stimulant. [. . .]

I kiss you with great sadness.

CHARLES

JEAN COCTEAU *(1889–1963)*

Cocteau's father committed suicide when the future artist was nine. He later wrote of a dream he had several times a week, from the age of ten on, set on a farm that was a mélange of several farms and the cockatoo (yes, in French, too, this sounds similar to his name) terrace of the Jardin d'Acclimatation. His dead father was not dead, but had turned into a Pré Catalan parrot "whose squawking," Cocteau remembers, "is always associated in my mind with the taste of foamy milk. In this dream my mother and I were about to sit down at a table . . . I knew that my mother knew, and that she didn't know I knew, and it was clear to me that she was trying to discover which of the birds it was that my father had turned into, and why he had turned into that bird. I awoke in tears because of the expression on her face: she was trying to smile." The following poem finds Jean himself with wings: he wrote his mother this quatrain for Christmas, 1918, saluting her motherhood of two sons who'd survived the war. (Cocteau himself saw plenty of action driving ambulances.)

Noël 1918

Nineteen nineteen brings to a close
Your war with its cruel discords.
One of your sons folds his wings
And the other feels his grow again.

*A*nd where were those growing wings of Jean Cocteau taking him? In 1916, he had written his mother, "I am trying to rise higher so as to be worthy of a following." The circus–music hall ballet *Parade*, Cocteau's collaboration with Erik Satie, Picasso, and Massine, was performed by Diaghilev's Ballets Russes in 1917—and set the tone in the arts for the postwar years.

Cocteau continued to fly, winning acclaim for his poetry, films, and further fabulous collaborations. His biographer Francis Steegmuller writes: "His sensibility to the extraordinary, the outstanding, was fostered by home and doting mother. He would see her leave for the theatre, 'bristling with aigrettes and swathed in red velvet. She would bring home programs covered with mysterious, important-sounding names. Sometimes I was sick—I had scarlet fever, I had measles like all children. She would give me the programs to read in bed, and I had toy theatres and would cut out scenery, and finally I caught an illness much more serious than scarlet fever or measles—what I call the red-and-gold disease: theatre-itis.'"

OSCAR WILDE (1854–1900)

FROM HIS MOTHER, LADY ESPERANZA WILDE

Lady Wilde, a writer who went by the rather heady pen name of Esperanza, was quick to offer her playwright son advice on everything from the titles for his plays (the most popular of which is The Importance of Being Earnest) *to his health. She was also quick to offer praise, as evidenced in part of a letter she sent to her flamboyant offspring in his pre-Earnest days, after he won the Newdigate prize at Oxford for a poem titled* Ravenna.

Oh Gloria! Gloria! Thank you a million times for the telegram. It is the first throb of joy I have had . . . Well, after all, we have *genius.* That is something. Attorneys can not take that away. Oh, I do hope you will have joy in your heart . . . You can now trust your intellect and know what it can do. I should so like to see the smile on your face now. This, at only twenty-two is a great thing.

THOMAS MOORE *(1779–1852)*

At twenty-two, Moore, who composed "The Last Rose of Summer" and other popular ballads, led a charmed life, and was fast becoming renowned for his poems, compositions, and expressive singing voice. Still, with all his success he missed news from home, particularly from his sister Catherine, who, judging from his complaints, was a lazy letter writer. Moore's reference to Thomas Little appears to have been a sort of pseudonym, or alter ego, for the composer, and here he playfully lavishes the same fictitious last name on his errant sibling.

Saturday, April 18, 1801

My dearest Mother,

I go on as usual; I am happy, careless, comical, everything I could wish; not very rich, nor yet quite poor. All I desire is that my dear ones at home may be as contented and easy in mind as I am. Tell me are you all happy and comfortable? I do not hear from you half often enough. The other day I dined with the Dowager Lady Donegal: We had music in the evening. Lady Charlotte Rawdon and I were obliged to sing my little glees three times. I go to Donington in about a week, I think: about that time my poems will all be printed. I suppose Captain A. told you they are coming out as 'The poetical works of the late Thos. Little, Esq.' You shall have a copy over immediately. I wrote a long letter to Miss Catherine Little this week. Make her answer me soon.

Ivan Turgenev (*1818–1883*)

FROM HIS MOTHER, VARVARA PETROVNA TURGENEV

When Turgenev's narrative poem Parasha *appeared to mixed reviews, his mother read it and wept tears of joy.*

Contrary to all the critics, I find the tone quite perfect, as well as the ending which, your brother tells me, has been criticized. It's sweet, delicate, discreet . . . I agree with the qualities singled out for praise in the *Annals of the Fatherland:* it is all perfectly true and despite the critics I am proud that my son has ideas like this, new ideas . . . I have been brought some wild strawberries. We countryfolk are fond of tangible things. So now your 'Parasha,' your tale, your poem, smells of wild strawberries.

THE GRAND TOUR
CONTINUES

JACK KEROUAC

I've been eating apple pie & ice cream all over Iowa & Nebraska

MARK TWAIN

*Our city lies in the midst of a desert of the purest, most unadulterated
and uncompromising sand*

WILLIAM FAULKNER

And — dont faint — I am growing a beard

HENRY JAMES

*I date the moment from which my mind rose erect in impartial might
to a little sail I took on the Thames*

GUSTAVE FLAUBERT

*You must be weeping at this moment, turning your poor beloved eyes
to the map*

THOMAS MOORE

This weather is only fit for poets, lovers, and murderers

JOSEPH SPENCE

*I hope you are furnished with a good map of Italy and a pair of jack-
boots to travel through it with me*

JACK KEROUAC *(1922–1969)*

Gabrielle Kerouac heard from her son throughout his trip across America, and in the case of one postcard, the note to Ma nearly matches a passage from his classic book On The Road, *which Jacky would finish writing in his room at home. Kerouac may write to his mom of apple pie, but from California he writes to Neal Cassady of his need for "food, rest, girls, dope, wine, beer, and Old Granddad." And in San Luis Obispo, where he settles for a while, he praises the view, the tranquility, "good sleep to the tune of crickets," and asks her to join him; his letter to Neal Cassady at the same time suggests joining him so he'd "have some kicks at yr. house instead of sitting naked in a San Luis Obispo railroad hotel room watching the high school girls come home at 2." The postcard genre would be refined in his collection of American haiku.*

> [July 24, 1947
> postmarked Shelton, Neb.]

Dear Ma—

I've been eating apple pie & ice cream all over Iowa & Nebraska, where the food is so good. Will be in Colorado tonight—and I'll write you a letter from Denver. Everything fine, money holding out.

> Love, Jacky XXX

P.S. You ought to see the *Cowboys* out here.

MARK TWAIN *(1835–1910)*

While most European young men seeking enlightenment in the nineteenth century and earlier went east to Italy or Greece for their Grand Tour, American humorist and satirist Mark Twain (a.k.a. Samuel Clemens) headed west for his, to Nevada Territory, a place sans Corinthian columns, grotesques, and Michelangelo frescoes. It was, instead, jumping with gold nuggets, desperadoes, gamblers, and jackrabbits—things that tended to move rather than stand still in ancient splendor. Unlike his creation the orphan Tom Sawyer, Twain was very much a fellow with a mother, and he wrote reams of descriptive letters to her.

[To Jane Lampton Clemens
26 October 1861, Carson City, Nev. Terr.
(Keokuk Gate City, 20 Nov 61)]
Carson City, Nevada Ter.,
October 26, '61.

DEAR MOTHER: You ask me in your last to tell you about the country—tell everything just as it is—no better and no worse— and *do* let nonsense alone. Very well, then, ma, since you wasted a considerable portion of your life in an unprofitable effort to teach me to tell the truth on all occasions, I will repay you by dealing strictly in facts just this once, and by avoiding that "nonsense" for which you seem to entertain a mild sort of horror.

Thus: "Gold Hill" (which is the name of the finest gold bearing quartz ledge in this vicinity,) sells at $5,000 a foot, cash down; 'Wildcat' isn't worth 10 cents. And thus: Nevada Territory is fabulously rich in gold, silver, copper, lead, coal, iron, quicksilver, marble, granite, chalk, slate, plaster of Paris (gypsum,) thieves, murderers, desperadoes, ladies, children, lawyers, Christians, gamblers,

Indians, Chinamen, Spaniards, sharpers, cuyotes, (pronounced ki-yo-ties,) preachers, poets and jackass-rabbits.

Furthermore: it never rains here, and the dew never falls. No flowers grow here, and no green thing gladdens the eye. The birds that fly over the land carry their provisions with them. Only the crow and raven tarry with us. Our city lies in the midst of a desert of the purest, most unadulterated and uncompromising sand—in which infernal soil nothing but that fag-end of vegetable creation, "sage-brush," is mean enough to grow. [. . .]

Behold, I have spoken the truth concerning this land. And now, for your other questions, which shall be answered tersely, promptly, and to the point: First—"Do I go to church every Sunday?" Answer—"Scasely." Second—"Have you a Church in Carson?" We have—a Catholic one—but, to use a fireman's expression, I believe "they don't run her now." We have also Protestant service nearly every Sabbath in the school house. Third—"Are there many ladies in Carson?" Multitudes—probably the handsomest in the world. Fourth—"Are the citizens generally moral and religious?" Prodigiously so. Fifth—"When my old friends ask me how you like Nevada, what reply shall I make?" Tell them I am *delighted* with it. It is the dustiest country on the face of the earth—but I rather like dust. And the days are very hot—but you know I am fond of hot days. And the nights are cold—but one always sleeps well under blankets. And it never rains here—but I despise a country where rain and mud are fashionable. [. . .] Tell them I never liked any country so well before—and my word for it, you will tell them the truth.

WILLIAM FAULKNER *(1897–1962)*

The author of Light in August, As I Lay Dying, *and* The Sound and the Fury, *William Faulkner, so often cited by Latin American and European writers as an inspiration and a strangely quintessential American writer—with his mythical Yoknapatawpha County and its snarled-up families and psyches—traveled through Italy, Switzerland, and France in 1925, spending an idyllic spell in Paris and writing letters home that express a tenderness and a pleasure in observing human character and interactions within another culture. An old man sailing his boat in a Parisian park, respected in his golden years, becomes the focus of some rich descriptive writing in two letters from Faulkner to his mother.*

Sunday 16 Aug 1925
Paris

. . . I came back toward home, stopping at the Luxembourg Gardens to watch the children sailing boats on the pool. There is a man rents boats—toy ones—and even grown people sail them, while their friends look on. There will be a big man looking like a butcher and mustached like a brigand, with all his family along, holding yacht races with another gang like his, while both wives and all the children cheer. And there was an old old man, bent and rheumatic, sailing a boat too. He hobbled along around the pool, but he couldnt keep up with his boat, so other people would very kindly stop it and send it back across to him.

The cathedral of Notre Dame is grand. Like the cathedral at Milan it is all covered with cardinals mitred like Assyrian kings, and knights leaning on long swords, and saints and angels, and beautiful naked Greek figures that have no religious significance what ever, and gargoyles—creatures with heads of goats and dogs, and claws and wings on men's bodies, all staring down in a jeering sardonic mirth. [. . .]

My french is improving—I get along quite well now. [. . .] And—dont faint—I am growing a beard.

Billy

Something [30 Aug.] August (Sunday) 1925

Dear Moms—

I wrote you, didn't I, about the old man who sails his boat in the pool in the Luxembourg gardens? He was there bright and early this morning when I came back from breakfast. It was a lovely day—(Paris weather is overcast and grey, as a rule)—the sun was out and it was crisp and cool. I saw him right away, hobbling along at top speed with his stick, sailing his boat while people watched him in a sort of jolly friendliness. [. . .] There was another old man in a blue yachting cap with a toy steam yacht. He was firing it up while about 6 people stood around giving him advice. They are really beautiful boats—well made, of fine wood, and all flagged and pennoned like big ones. Think of a country where an old man, if he wants to, can spend his whole time with toy ships, and no one to call him crazy or make fun of him! In America they laugh at him if he drives a car even, if he does anything except play checkers and sleep in the courthouse yard.

. . . The French treat their children like they were grown people, and even 5 year old children are as polite as grown people. And here when you pay your fare on a street car the conductor says 'Thank you.' And as for buying something in a store—its like going to a reception. Like this—

Good day, sir.
Good day, madam.
What will you have, sir?
Tooth paste, if you please, madam.
Thank you, sir. (gives you the toothpaste) Here it is, sir. Thank you.
Thank you, madam (give her a 5 franc note)
Thank you, sir (takes the note: gives you the change) Thank you, sir.
Thank you, madam (you take the change) Good day, madam.
Farewell, sir.
Good day, sirs (to every one else in the shop)
Good day, sir (they reply. You go out.)

HENRY JAMES *(1843–1916)*

In his childhood, Henry James lurched around Europe with the rest of his brilliant, lively, family — one three-year stay deeply impressed him and gave him his first sense of art as life. As a young man, with the James family well established in Cambridge and Henry securely at home in literature, the American writer sprung himself free from New England to return to England and the Continent for a year of fervent exploration, setting the scene for himself where so much of his future fiction would take place: The Golden Bowl, Daisy Miller, The Ambassadors, *and* The Turn of the Screw. *As much at home on the Sceptered Isle as anywhere, James was in England when Queen Victoria died, and he mused, "We all feel a bit motherless today."*

7 Half Moon St., W.

March 26, 1869.

My dearest Mother,

. . . If I were in anything like working order now, I should be very sorry to leave England. I should like to settle down for a year and expose my body to the English climate and my mind to English institutions. But a truce to this cheap discursive stuff. I date the moment from which my mind rose erect in impartial might to a little sail I took on the Thames the other day in one of the little penny steamers which shoot along its dirty bosom. It was a grey, raw English day, and the banks of the river, as far as I went, were hideous. Nevertheless I enjoyed it. [. . .] The next day I went with several of the Nortons to dine at Ruskin's, out of town. [. . .] Ruskin himself is a very simple matter. In face, in manner, in talk, in mind, he is weakness pure and simple. I use the word, not invidiously, but scientifically. He has the beauties of his defects; but to see him only confirms the impression given by his writing, that he has been scared back by the grim face of reality into the world of unreason and illusion, and that he wanders there without a compass and a guide—or any light save the fitful flashes of his beautiful genius. The dinner was very nice and easy, owing in a great manner to Ruskin's two charming young nieces who live with him—one a lovely young Irish girl with a rich virginal brogue—a creature of a truly delightful British maiden simplicity—and the other a nice Scotch lass, who keeps house for him. But I confess, cold-blooded villain that I am, that what I most enjoyed was a portrait by Titian— an old doge, a work of transcendent beauty and elegance, such as to give one a new sense of the meaning of art. . . . But, dearest mammy, I must pull up. Pile in scraps of news. Osculate my sister most passionately. Likewise my aunt. Be assured of my sentiments and present them to my father and brother.

Thy HENRY jr.

GUSTAVE FLAUBERT *(1821–1880)*

In October of 1849, on 27,500 francs his mother had given him, Gustave Flaubert set out for the Middle East on the journey he'd dreamed of—an adventure that would infuse his exotic novel Salammbô. *The last night in Paris before their departure, his traveling companion Maxime Du Camp found him sobbing on the floor in front of the fire: "I shall never see my mother again! I shall never see my own country again! This journey is too long, too far; it's tempting fate! What madness! Why are we going?" Once on their way, Flaubert wrote his mother almost every day, addressing her as his "poor old darling." Aboard the packet* Le Nil *from Marseilles, Flaubert was pleased to find himself a good sailor. And the second letter excerpted here was written at the end of March when he had gone up the Nile as far as possible.*

I don't know what it is about me, but I am adored on board. The watery element is so flattering to my physiognomy, it seems, that these gentlemen [the crew] call me Papa Flaubert. You see, my poor old dear, that things are off to a good start.

. . . Sometimes I have a craving to see you that grips me all of a sudden like cramps of tenderness. At night before falling asleep I think of you fondly, and every morning when I wake up, you are the first thing that comes into my mind. . . . I can still see you leaning on your elbow with your chin in your hand, dreaming with your kind, sad air. [. . .] You may be weeping at this moment, turning your poor beloved eyes to the map, which means nothing to you but an empty space in which your son is lost. [. . .]

THOMAS MOORE *(1779-1852)*

Having just returned from a trip to Bermuda, Moore maintains his festive mood and busy social schedule despite dark English weather, dashing off lines to his mother back in Ireland. His description of illuminated walks in the second epistle pulls us out of the November gloom and into the home of acclaimed British actress Sarah Siddons, just one of the many celebrities the Irish songsmith met within his stellar circle of acquaintances.

Nov. 8. 1805

My dearest Mother,

This weather is only fit for poets, lovers, and murderers: there is hardly light enough to pursue any other calling. It is now but four o'clock, and I can scarcely see to write a line. I am just going to dine third to Rogers and Cumberland: a good poetical step-ladder we make—the former is past forty and the latter past seventy.

I wish I could hope to dance at Eliza A.'s ball. I have not capered much since I left Bermuda; though I forget myself—at Tunbridge, my toe had a few fantastic sallies. God bless you all, dears, and good friends. Your own,

Tom.

Donington
Monday [November, 1805?]

My dearest Mother,

[. . .] I was at a beautiful little fête champêtre at Mrs. Siddons's cottage on Saturday evening: it was the most fairy scene I ever witnessed; and even the duchesses and countesses looked romantic in the illuminated walks. Bless you, darling mother. Ever your own,

Tom.

JOSEPH SPENCE *(1699–1768)*

Before Joseph Spence set out on his first Grand Tour, he was advised by the Dean of Petersborough that he would learn to speak the language of each country he visited much better from conversing with the ladies, "who are the best for it." He paid attention to them even when they were locked up, as we see during this visit to Milan. He reports here on matters he knew would interest his mother, saving his more arcane, classical, and scholarly observations for his books Observations, Polymetis, *and* Crito. *One's heart goes out to the motherless children (as his obviously did) he enountered in the foundling ward. Spence himself rejoiced in having a mother and, as a bachelor, in keeping house with her. Horace Walpole said that Spence "fondles an old mother in imitation of Pope"—Alexander Pope, that is, who was so instrumental in facilitating Spence's first felicitous tour.*

Milan,
November 5, 1731

Dear Mother,

I hope you are furnished with a good map of Italy and a pair of jackboots to travel through it with me. I left you in my last at Turin. After the pleasures of that delicious city we went to Milan. [. . .]

[. . .] The women do not only keep generally within, but appear too very rarely in the shops or any public part of their own houses. They keep mostly in their own chamber, and their chief diversion is looking out of [the] window. Even when they do that, you must not expect to see their faces: there's a sort of wooden lattice (they call them 'jealousies') that generally hangs down all over the outside of the window, 'tis made movable to about half a foot before them; there they poke out their heads and see about them without being fairly seen. By what one could discover of them, I believe there were several faces among them that deserved better usage.

The dress of the head is especially becoming. The common people wear nothing upon their heads: their hair is twisted in two long braids behind. These braids are then drawn round and round a silver bodkin on the top of their heads and looks like a natural crown of hair—the rest they set very prettily to the face, and if they have any ornament at all on the head 'tis two or three real rosebuds or a sprig of jessamin. The ladies come very often near this, or if they go farther 'tis often nothing but a little cap, all of short red ribbons, and for the graver gentry black. [. . .]

One of the things that I have seen with the greatest pleasure at Milan was the Grand Hospital. [. . .] In one square are religious women, in another the sick, in another the decrepit, and in a fourth children that come by chance into the world, etc. [. . .] The number of the bastards upon the spot there, or now prenticed with the hospital money, amounts to between eleven or twelve thousand. In a modest computation they have about ten fresh ones come in every week. We were in the chamber of infants, and I never saw anything that pleased me more. There were between fifty and sixty little creatures perhaps, all from a day or two to seven or eight weeks old, and about ten neat nurses in the room that seemed as busy and as pleased in taking care of them as could be. Above half the chits were asleep in little long beds with bolsters at both ends, and sometimes you'd see two little heads together at each end. Some were feeding and scarce anyone whimpering, for they manage them extremely carefully and well. I believe most of the nurses had been of the same breed themselves, and as they grew up were taught to take care of their new little cousins as they came in. We have something of this kind in all the great cities where I have been: there is a noble one in particular at Venice, and before it was established they said they used to find numbers of little children floating in their canals, some every morning: horrible sight, which is now put an end to. Though the hospital at Milan [. . .] is so rich, there are still people continually leaving money to it. They have a great hall with the pictures of their benefactors in it, among which there is one in a shabby dress who was a small coalman, but managed his gains so well that he died worth a hundred thousand crowns and left them all to the hospital. With hearty services to all friends, I wish you and Belle a happy New year, and am ever

Your affectionate and dutiful

Jo: Spence

High Intensity

Richard Wagner

> It is sad and distressing that I am obliged to use such strong language,
> but our good mama is utter hell for everyone around her

Nikolai Gogol

> How could you think that a son of such angelic parents could become
> a monster in whom not a single virtuous trait was left!

Marcel Proust

> Such thoughts are less painful when we are near one another

Mikhail Bulgakov

> I dream of just one thing: of surviving the winter

Thomas Moore

> I am almost growing anxious from this silence

Kaethe Kollwitz to her son

> Why does work help me in these times?

VANESSA BELL TO HER SISTER

I am only working at small things which matter to no one but myself

JEAN COCTEAU

If some kind person should say to you, "Isn't your son the leader of a Negro jazz band?" answer: "Yes. We think it's the best job he's ever had . . ."

RICHARD WAGNER *(1813–1883)*

With a fondness for pink underwear, red socks, and chamois shirts—not to mention dwarfs, dragons, and Rhinemaidens—Prussian composer Richard Wagner immersed not only his operas, such as the Ring cycle and Tann-häuser, but also his life in the high drama of extremes and excesses. His contrasting feelings about people ricocheted from high to low, even his feelings toward his mother, whom he once dreamed was the queen of Prussia (while Tennessee Williams had visions of his mother as a Prussian army officer in drag). In the following letter, written when he was twenty-three, Wagner puts mother love on the highest pedestal (you can almost hear the letter scored for orchestra, with tender strings swelling and a regal brass section climbing and creating a throne of glowing notes). But in a letter to his sister Cecilie, he sticks his mother with Siegfried's sword and twists it a little, writing, "It is sad and distressing that I am obliged to use such strong language, but our good mama is utter hell for everyone around her." He deplores her "really offensive avarice and egoism which we were exposed to ad nauseam *in various trivial ways." Maybe, too, she deprived him of vibrant socks and flaming knickers at a tender age.*

[Johanna Rosine Geyer, Leipzig]
Carlsbad, 25 July 1835

Only you, dearest mother, do I still recall with feelings of the most heartfelt love and deepest emotion;—I know only too well that children go their own way—they think only of themselves & their future, and of the people around them who provide a link between the two; that is how it is & it is something I feel myself, there is a time when separation becomes inevitable;—we then conduct our reciprocal relationships solely from a standpoint of superficiality; we become diplomats joined together by ties of friendship,—we remain silent where it seems politic to do so,—and speak when our view of the affair demands it, and we speak most of all when we are separated from each other. Ah, but how greatly a mother's love transcends all that! I think I, too, am one of those people who cannot always say what they feel in their hearts at a given moment,— otherwise you would often have encountered a more tender-hearted side to my nature. But my feelings remain the same,—& look mother, now that I am no longer beside you, I am overcome by feelings of gratitude for the glorious love of which you recently gave your son such heartfelt and earnest proofs, so much so that I might well be tempted to write and speak of them in the most tender tones of a lover addressing his beloved. Ah, but far greater— is not a mother's love far greater, far more unsullied than that other love?—No, I do not intend to wax philosophical here,—I wish only to thank you, & to thank you yet again,—I wish I could enumerate all the individual tokens of your love for which I have cause to be grateful,—but it would take too long to do so. Yet I know that there is no heart which follows my every move with such sincere interest & such solicitous concern as does your own,—nay, it is perhaps the only heart that watches over my every step,—& not with the intention of passing unfeeling judgement on all that I do,—no, rather it is your wish to include me in your prayers. Were you not the only one to remain unflinchingly loyal to me, when others, judging me simply by external events, turned their back on me with a philosophical gesture of dismissal? I should be intemperately presumptuous if I were to demand the same degree of love from everyone, I know well enough that that is not possible—I know that for myself.—Everything comes straight from your heart, from your dear, kind heart, which I pray to God may always remain well disposed towards me,—for I know that if all else fails, it will always remain my final & dearest refuge. Oh mother, if you were to die prematurely, before I could give you adequate proof that your love had been bestowed upon a noble recipient, whose gratitude knows no bounds! No, that cannot be, you must live to enjoy many more fine fruits of your love!—Ah, when I recall the final week we spent together! It is a source of perfect consolation & comfort to me to recall to mind the many demonstrations of your loving kindness! My dear, dear mother,— how pitiable I should be if my feelings towards you were ever to grow cold!—

NIKOLAI GOGOL *(1809–1852)*

Maria Gogol, née Kosiarowska, gave interviews after Gogol's death in which she claimed that her son had invented the steam engine and had planned the railroad network that was being constructed all over Russia in the 1850s. During his life she credited him with works by various French and Russian authors, including several trashy pulp novels. Today he is rightly remembered for his unique narration in short stories such as "The Overcoat" and "The Nose," and his dark, comic novel Dead Souls, awrithe with unforgettable images and one of literature's oddest protagonists, Chichikov.

Letters to his mother make up the bulk of Gogol's surviving correspondence, and are overcoated with affection, sugar, and esteem, all the while rolling in lies. He addresses her in variations ranging from the babyish to the mawkishly grandiloquent: Drazhaishay mamen'ka *("My Most Precious Mommy");* Velikodushnay mater *("Oh Magnanimous Mater"). When his mother pieced together letters from her son in Germany explaining his sudden departure for Lübeck (on money she'd sent him to pay off a mortgage)— letters referring to his love affair with a lofty woman and to his seeking a cure for a rash on his face and arms—and concluded that Gogol had contracted a venereal disease, Gogol replied:*

[24 September 1829]
With horror I read your letter, mailed on September 6. I could expect everything from you: deserved reproaches, much too kind to me, just indignation and everything else that my ill-considered act could provoke, but *this* I couldn't expect. How could you, dearest mommy, ever think that I had fallen victim to the vilest debauchery, that I find myself on the lowest rung of human degradation! How could you, finally, resolve yourself to ascribe to me a disease, the very thought of which has always made my very thoughts quiver with horror! for the first, and may God grant that it be the last, time in my life, I had received such a terrifying letter. It seemed as if I was hearing a malediction. How could you think that a son of such angelic parents could become a monster in whom not a single virtuous trait was left! [. . .] But I am ready to answer to God that I have not committed even a single depraved exploit; my morality is incomparably more pure than it was at school and at home. As for drunkenness, I never had that habit. At home I used to drink wine, but I do not remember having any here. [. . .]

Is that my mother sitting there at her window? Mother dear, save your poor son! Shed a tear upon his aching head. See, how they torture him. Press the poor orphan to your heart. There is no place for him in the whole wide world! He is a hunted creature. Mother dear, take pity on your sick little child. . . . And by the way, gentlemen, do you know that the Bey of Algiers has a round lump growing right under his nose?

—Nikolai Gogol, *Diary of a Madman*
from Vladimir Nabokov, *Nikolai Gogol*

MARCEL PROUST (*1871–1922*)

Proust, who devoted most of his adult life to exploring the layers and textures of time, and the emotions, sensations, and telling details that saturate it with significance, here explores these themes in a personal and familial vein, remembering the life and death of his father—before the letter ends in a flurry of sneezes.

Saturday evening [24 September 1904]

My dear little Mama,

It seems to me that I think of you more tenderly if possible (though it isn't) today the 24th of September. Each time this day comes round, although all the thoughts accumulated hour by hour since the first day should make the time that has already gone by seem so terribly long, the habit of constantly looking back to that day and to all the happiness that preceded it, the habit of regarding everything that has happened since as a sort of mechanical nightmare, means that on the contrary it seems like yesterday and one has to work out the dates to convince oneself that it's already ten months ago, that one has already been unhappy too long, that there are still many long years of unhappiness ahead, that for ten whole months my poor little Papa has ceased to enjoy anything, no longer knows the sweetness of life. Such thoughts are less painful when we are near one another but when, as we two are, one is linked by a sort of wireless telegraphy, whether more or less near or more or less far one is always in close communion, always side by side. [. . .]

I'm still very out of sorts. I came home last night without having an attack and went to bed more or less in the same state as if I hadn't gone out. On the other hand I had a protracted attack, though without spasms, in the morning which obliged me to go back to sleep very late and to get up rather hurriedly which brought on my discomfort again [...]

I'm very well at the moment of writing and on the whole it's only the contrast with the well-being I felt only a week ago that irritates me. But I'm not suffering at all. [...] Mme Lemaire writes to Reynaldo to ask him if I've had 'the courage to go away for treatment etc.', and her daughter to say that her mother makes life unbearable for her. That's something I can never say of my dear little Mama! who would be so pleased to see me un-suffocated as on the whole I am, since my attack this morning was the only one, and as I say not at all violent; for instance, I sneezed quite a lot as I used to when I got up in the daytime. [...]

MIKHAIL BULGAKOV (1891–1940)

Mikhail Bulgakov's coruscating novel The Master and Margarita *was not published until twenty-five years after his death, whereupon it became one of the greatest marvels of twentieth-century literature. Some of its radiance emanates from a diabolical source, reminding us that Lucifer, alight, was a bad boy from heaven. Bulgakov was actually a doctor, but as this desperate letter shows, he did other things to barely survive and buy his wife shoes. His involvement with the theater led to a lesser, unfinished novel,* Black Snow, *in which Stanislavsky, with whom he had a falling-out over Bulgakov's play* Moliére, *is a less than exalted character. This letter comes from a collection of diaries and letters that took as its title one of Bulgakov's guiding principles, expressing his belief in the supremacy and endurance of art:* Manuscripts Don't Burn.

[17 November 1921]
[From Moscow to Kiev]

Dear Mama,

[...] I very much regret that in a short letter I cannot communicate to you a detailed picture of what Moscow is like at the moment. Briefly, I can say that a furious battle is going on for survival and to adapt to the new conditions of life. [. . .] Taska and I are already more or less managing to eat this month, we've stocked up with potatoes, she's got her shoes mended, we've begun to buy firewood, and so on.

You have to work not just normally, but frenetically. From morning to night every day without a break. All Soviet institutions are being turned inside out and people are getting the chop. [. . .]

[. . .] I have a huge number of acquaintances in journalism, in the theatre and simply in business. That means a great deal in present-day Moscow, which is making the transition to a new kind of life such as it has not witnessed for a long time: savage competition, bustle, the need to show your initiative and so on. It is impossible to live outside that life, you would simply perish. I have no wish to be among the number of those who perish.

Taska is looking for a job as a sales assistant, which is very difficult since the whole of Moscow is still naked and barefoot and is trading ephemerally; for the most part they're using their own strengths and resources, and employing just their own people. Poor Taska is having to exert all her strength to grind rye using an axe-head, and to prepare meals out of all sorts of rubbish. But she's doing very well! [. . .]

In Moscow they count only in hundreds of thousands or in millions. Black bread is 4,600 roubles a pound, white is 14,000. And the prices are rising and rising! The shops are full of goods, but what can you buy! The theatres are full, but yesterday as I was passing by the Bolshoy [. . .] the touts were selling tickets for 75,100 and 150 thousand roubles! In Moscow there is everything: shoes, cloth, meat, caviare, preserves, delicacies, everything! Cafés are opening, they're sprouting like mushrooms. And everywhere hundreds of thousands of roubles, hundreds! Hundreds! There is the buzzing of a wave of speculation.

I dream of just one thing: of surviving the winter, of not succumbing in December, which will be the hardest month, I reckon. Taska's support is invaluable to me: given the enormous distances that I have to run around (literally) over the whole of Moscow, she saves me a great deal of energy and strength by feeding me and leaving for me to do only those things that she can really not do herself: chopping wood in the evening and fetching potatoes in the morning.

We both go around Moscow in our light coats. For that reason I somehow walk about sideways on (I don't know why, my left side feels the draught more). I dream of getting Tatyana warm footwear. She hasn't got a thing except her shoes.

THOMAS MOORE (*1779–1852*)

Despite his full and active life in England, popular songwriter Moore missed word from his family in Ireland with a palpable impatience and some real concern, particularly faulting his sister Catherine for neglect. His mother was surely the most sympathetic listener to complain to of his empty postbox.

[Donington Park]
May 21, 1801.

I am now more than three weeks at Donington, and in that time have received but one short letter from home—this is not fair. I am sure my regularity ought to be a little better rewarded. My father I excuse. I trust and hope from my soul he has business to keep him from writing; but the little idle gipsy, Catherine, who can have no other employment than to improve herself, ought surely to make correspondence with me one medium of that improvement. I am almost growing anxious from this silence, to me so very gloomy; and I sometimes dread that all is not right at home, or the common occupations of the day could never so interrupt your writing to me. Tell me truth, my darling mother, are you all happy and in health? Make Catherine write to me oftener: there are a thousand little nothings at the day's news which I should like to hear. . . .

KAETHE KOLLWITZ (1867–1945)

TO HER SON HANS KOLLWITZ

Kaethe Kollwitz of Germany and Vanessa Bell of England were both artists who lost sons to war—Kaethe her youngest, Peter, in World War I on the German side, and Vanessa her eldest, Julian, in the Spanish Civil War. The devastating experience affected them differently. Kaethe, who ironically embraced themes of human suffering in her paintings, plunged into her work, as recorded in a letter to her son Hans. Vanessa, a member of the free-thinking Bloomsbury set, was paralyzed by grief, and could concentrate only on casual projects, as evidenced in a letter to her sister, Virginia Woolf.

Sunday, February 21, 1915

My dear Hans! [. . .] Why does work help me in these times? It is not enough to say that it relaxes me very much. It is simply that it is a task I may not shirk. As you, the children of my body, have been my tasks, so too are my other works. Perhaps that sounds as though I meant that I would be depriving humanity of something if I stopped working. In a certain sense—yes. Because this is my post and I may not leave it until I have made my talent bear interest. Everyone who is vouchsafed life has the obligation of carrying out to the last item the plan laid down for him. Then he may go. Probably that's the point at which most people die. Peter was "seed for the planting which must not be ground." [. . .]

I am not seed for the planting. I have only the task of nurturing the seed placed in me. And you, my Hans? May you have been born for life after all! You must have been, and you must believe in it.

VANESSA BELL *(1879–1961)*

TO HER SISTER, VIRGINIA WOOLF

In an effort to help Vanessa Bell recover from the loss of her son Julian, her sister Virginia Woolf had tried to commission her to paint Clive Bell's portrait.

Sept. 9 [1937]

Charleston

. . . I don't think I can paint portraits at present. It needs a special kind of effort which I don't think I'm capable of. Sketching Angelica is different, as she's not sitting specially to me. But I couldn't settle down to paint Clive, or anyone, seriously as a matter of business at present, flattered though I am by the notion. It's foolish I know, but I can't help it. I'm only working at small things which matter to no one but myself.

Adrian is coming I believe the weekend after next, and Angus some day next week. So no more solitude.

Your

VB

JEAN COCTEAU (*1889–1963*)

Poor Madame Cocteau! As a teenager, Jean played tricks on her, as did his Surrealist friends when they were all apparently grown up. On a trip with his mother, returning by train to Paris from Switzerland, Jean threatened to throw a terrible tantrum if she didn't hide under her dress the box of cigars he'd insisted she buy their servant, Auguste. When they were approached with inquiries by the customs inspector at the border, Jean gave her away: "The lady is hiding a box of cigars under her dress." Later, some of his Surrealist copains would occasionally call Madame Cocteau and inform her that her son had died.

March 30, 1921

Ma chérie,

My pleasant stay here is quite shot to pieces. Your letter has come—the letter that I now know so well and that would inevitably arrive even were I to go as far as Texas for a little quiet.

When will you stop seeing me through the eyes of the cheap press?

To be specific:

1. The bar [Gaya]. A charming place, easy, where we can all meet without going to cafés like the artists of a generation ago. Lautrec himself tried to have something of the kind. Wiener and his Negro play very well indeed. Stravinsky has lent me his drum, and I play it as often as I can as relaxation—I love the instrument for various reasons, poetry not excluded.

2. The "hyenas" you speak of invent whatever they don't see— so what they say makes no difference.

3. Radiguet was supposed to leave. It was I who prevailed on him to stay. I admire and respect him, and nothing and *nobody* can

change my opinion, for my own first rule is not to commit the injustice that the pious practice every day of their lives. [. . .]

4. As for what you term my having "wasted a winter"—I wrote and prepared for *Mariés:* a mere nothing for you, perhaps, but for me something quite considerable. I brought off the triumph of *Parade.* I published *Escales* with Lhote—a book that I haven't even shown you, knowing that you would dislike it. I was given a commission by Diaghilev. I don't mention my bust by Lipchitz, or the poems I wrote for the volume I am finishing here, in addition to the *Discours* and a number of other activities that would fill *ten* winters for anybody else.

You pray a good deal. But watch out: one thing prayer does is to keep you from analyzing things and seeing them as they really are. Kindness and encouragement from you would help me more than a candle. But I've given up all hope of this, and "my heart is broken," as you would put it. . . .

"Pull yourself together," you say? That's a good one. Don't you realize yet that I spend my life disengaging myself from my instincts, keeping them under observation, sorting them as they emerge, and then taming them for my advantage? Such is the discipline that you never manage to understand, the discipline that is entirely of my own creation, like everything I do. NEVER AGAIN expect me to do anything in a conventional way. ONCE AND FOR ALL.

. . . If some kind person should say to you, "Isn't your son the leader of a Negro jazz band?" answer: "Yes. We think it's the best job he's ever had, and he is resigned to it. As a mater of fact he's even beginning to like it. . . ."

SWEET EFFUSIONS

A. E. HOUSMAN

The violets also were very sweet: I don't know whether St. Paul used to enclose violets

ELVIS PRESLEY

Hi Babies

MARCEL PROUST'S MOTHER

But above all no more of that looking like a Frankish king—your hair gets in my eyes when I think of you

HENRI DE TOULOUSE-LAUTREC

I squeeze your little paw

NIKOS KAZANTZAKIS

"I got a letter from home!" I shouted to him. "From my mother and my sisters. That's what's come over me!"

LEO TOLSTOY

I'm crying again. Why do I cry when I think of you?

A. E. Housman *(1859–1936)*

By the time of this letter, Housman had moved from the precocious deism of his childhood to atheism, a dramatic background for this tableau of St. Paul and the cherub aspiring to be God—until Lucifer offers the added allure of a tail. At this point, Housman was making his mark with scholarly classical writings, after five years of frustrations in both his academic and emotional life, the latter because his homosexual inclinations were at odds with his conventional morality.

29 March 1885
82 Talbot Road, Bayswater

My dear Mamma,

I was delighted to get your long letter on the 26th: it was quite the best epistle I have ever seen, with the possible exception of the second of the apostle Paul to the Corinthians. The violets also were very sweet: I don't know whether St. Paul used to enclose violets. [. . .] Clemence and Laurence sent me a postcard with a very lovely drawing on the back, representing Cherubim and Seraphim continually crying, and an inscription in Spanish or Portuguese, I think. [. . .]

The juvenile son of a friend of mine at the Office has the loftiest ambition I ever heard tell of. When he goes to heaven, which he regards as a dead certainty, he wants to be *God,* and is keenly mortified to learn that it is not probable he will. However his aspirations are now turning into another channel: it has come to his knowledge, through the housemaid, that the devil has horns and a tail; and in comparison with these decorations the glories of heaven have lost their attractiveness. [. . .]

[. . .] I remain your loving son

A. E. Housman

Elvis Presley *(1935–1977)*

Although his song "Return to Sender," delivered in the style of Jackie Wilson, is about writing and repeatedly posting a letter to a spatting sweetheart, Elvis—Southern belle (with mascara) and enfant terrible*—wrote very few letters in his life, even to his mother, Gladys. This telegram to his parents from Houston in the late fifties, when he was first performing in the South with backup musicians Bill and Scotty and making some regular money, sings of his fabled devotion and generosity.*

HI BABIES. HERE'S THE MONEY TO PAY THE BILLS. DON'T TELL NO ONE HOW MUCH I SENT I WILL SEND MORE NEXT WEEK. THERE IS A CARD IN THE MAIL. LOVE ELVIS.

We await nothing more than you to preside over a familial veal flanked with wild lettuces. . . . Don't forget the jam.
        —Henri de Toulouse-Lautrec

M A R C E L   P R O U S T   *(1 8 7 1 – 1 9 2 2)*

FROM HIS MOTHER, JEANNE PROUST

Marcel was obviously Madame Proust's favorite: he was "mon petit loup," *my little wolf, while Robert (whom Maman Proust, mischievously teasing, called Proustovich in later letters to Marcel) was always* "mon autre loup," *my other wolf. Marcel was not the only boy or man in France whose maman called her son "my little wolf."*

> Hôtel des Bains, Dieppe
> Sunday 25 [September 1904]

My darling,

Your letter only arrived this morning. I'm glad. There isn't another delivery on Sunday and if I had eaten your letter yesterday I would have had to fast today! [. . .] Your stationer for cards is Brou 12 boulevard Malesherbes. He can give you some in 24 hours (he's very helpful). But I think it would be better to use your block (which is fine for white cards), and without going to the unnecessary expense of a new block, ask them to engrave a hundred cards [. . .] You are wrong, darling, your letters are all charming, all appreciated by me as I appreciate my little pet from every point of view. Besides, 'even when the bird is on the move'. . . and again this morning I've gleaned some golden corn. Forain very funny, Tristan Bernard very witty and standing out above all the pretentious nonsense — such as Jules Renard!! Roujon's very 'Parisian' patronage of Mme de Sévigné deserved the punishment advocated by your uncle. My darling don't send me anything and calm everyone's zeal and forbid all consignments of any kind. [. . .]

> A thousand kisses my darling boy,
> J. Proust

Do look after your appearance. If you have to get dressed in the daytime make sure your clothes are immaculate. But above all no more of that looking like a Frankish king—your hair gets in my eyes when I think of you. I hope by the time I finish this you'll have had it done. . . .

HENRI DE TOULOUSE-LAUTREC (*1864–1901*)

It would be unforgivable to exclude this letter Toulouse-Lautrec wrote to his Aunt Joséphine's dog, tendering his felicitations upon the birth of her puppies, his acknowledgment of the great gifts and demands of motherhood, and a solicitous warning not to sink her maternal teeth into Mélanie, the housekeeper. Here, he displayed powers of observation that would not fail him later amid the night life of Montmartre.

Le Bosc
[1880]

Dear Madam,

As your nice letter yesterday announced, maternity's joys are yours once again. There you are, once again the head of a family; grave responsibilities weighing down your curly little head. What care you will have to lavish on these warm and rosy little creatures, feebly stirring their tiny little paws at the bottom of your basket. I'm sure your nice mistress and Mélanie will help you with this difficult task and that they will make as much and even more fuss over your children as you yourself. I also know you must have a crazy urge to eat the aforesaid Mélanie when she wants to touch your progeny and that the echoes of your G-r-r-r-G-r-r-r will resound in the living-room.

So, first of all, I implore you not to eat all of the above-mentioned Mélanie and to leave at least a little piece of her to care for your nice mistress; second, to lick your babies very thoroughly, so that the good people of Castelnau will be able to raise their hands to heaven and say, amid tears of emotion, 'Oh God, they're just like their mother!'

In closing I send you my heartfelt congratulations, and pray you to lick your mistress's hand for me.

I squeeze your little paw,

Henri de Toulouse-Lautrec

P. S. Remember to give my best to Flavie, Mélanie, and Benjamin

Nikos Kazantzakis *(1885–1957)*

Here again is our bountiful, blazing Greek bohème, filling a Paris street with laughter as his student sojourn continues. Moré, the word by which his countryman greets him, is Greek for "dear fellow," and that is how we think of him, too, knowing him through these letters.

Paris

spring, 1908

Darling Mother, Anestasia and Eleni,

. . . Last night I went to bed late. . . . We'd gone to a café, shouting away, and the French people staring at us. I was one of the first to shout and laugh. A student friend of mine came to Paris the other day, and he didn't know I was here. Suddenly I saw him running like mad through the crowd, shouting "Niko!" I stood still. "Moré, you here!" he said. "I heard you laughing from the other end of the street, and I said, No one else can laugh like that. And here you are!" . . .

Paris [no date]
. . . I have no greater joy than to get a letter from you. Really,
many times I say to myself that no one in the world loves his
mother and his sisters as much as I do. The other day, after getting
your letter, I went to the University. A friend of mine said to me
the moment he saw me: "What's wrong with you? What's come
over you?" "I got a letter from home!" I shouted to him. "From my
mother and sisters. That's what's come over me!" . . .

LEO TOLSTOY *(1828–1910)*

*Although he lost his mother at the age of two, Leo, or Lev, Tolstoy found filial
felicity with another woman almost straightaway—a woman who'd loved his
father before his marriage, then turned down his proposal after his wife's death,
but accepted the other one—to be a mother to his children. When Nikolay
Tolstoy himself died a year later, Tatyana Alexandrovna Yergolskaya assumed
full responsibility for the family. This arrangement didn't last throughout Leo's
childhood, as the children were later sent to live with their new guardian in
Kazan, but Tolstoy's affection was lasting indeed, as his many letters to Tante
Toinette attest. Toinette, whose French was more active than her Russian,
encouraged Tolstoy to "faire des romans," write novels, long before he'd written
to publish, and once he got started, she admired the output that included
Anna Karenina, and kept cheering him on. After his marriage, she came to
live at Yasnaya Polyana until her death in 1874, although she lived on as
Sonya of War and Peace. More than a hundred letters from Tolstoy to Tante
Toinette remain, many written, as these, from the Caucasus, where he was
stationed with the army.*

Mozdok, a posting-station half-way from Tiflis,
12 January 1852

Dear Aunt,

[...] in thinking of the happiness in store for me. This is how I picture it to myself. After an unspecified number of years I am at [Yasnaya], neither young nor old—my affairs are in order, I have no anxieties, no worries—and you still live at [Yasnaya] too. You have aged a little, but are still fresh and in good health. We lead the life that we used to lead; I work in the morning, but we see each other almost the whole day; we have dinner; in the evening I read to you something that doesn't bore you; then we talk. I tell you of my life in the Caucasus, you talk to me of your memories—of my father and mother; you tell me [frightening stories] that we once listened to with startled eyes and gaping mouths. We recall the people who were dear to us and who are now no more; you will weep; I will do the same; but these tears will be sweet. [...] We won't have any friends—no one will come and bore us and talk gossip. It's a beautiful dream, but it's still not all that I allow myself to dream of. I am married—my wife is a sweet, good, affectionate person; she loves you in the same way as I do. We have children who call you 'grandmama'; you live in the big house, upstairs—the same room that grandmama used to live in; the whole house is as it was in papa's time, and we begin the same life again, only changing roles; you take the role of grandmama, but you are even better; I take the role of papa, but I despair of ever deserving it; my wife, that of mama; the children—our own; [...] But we shan't have anyone to take the role that you have played in our family. Never shall we find a soul as beautiful or as affectionate as yours. You will have no successor. There will be three new persons who will appear on the scene from time to time—my brothers—especially the one who will often be with us—Nikolay—an old bachelor, bald, retired from service, as noble as ever.

[I imagine how, as in the old days, he will tell the children fairy stories of his own invention; how the children will kiss his greasy (but deserving) hands; how he will play with them; how my wife will go to the trouble to make him his favourite meal; how he and I will recall common memories of time long past; how you will sit in your usual place and listen to us with pleasure; how, as before, you will call us old men 'Lyovochka and Nikolenka', and will scold me for eating with my fingers, and him for not having clean hands.]

If they made me Emperor of Russia, if they gave me Peru, in a word if a fairy came with her wand to ask me what I desired; my hand on my heart, I would reply that my only desire is for this to become a reality. [. . .] Dear Aunt, tell me: would you be happy? All that could come to pass, and hope is such a sweet thing.

I'm crying again. Why do I cry when I think of you? They are tears of happiness—I am happy to be able to love you. If every misfortune were to befall me, I would never call myself completely unhappy as long as you existed. [. . .] Goodbye, dear Aunt; in a few days I hope to see Nikolay again, and I will write to you then.

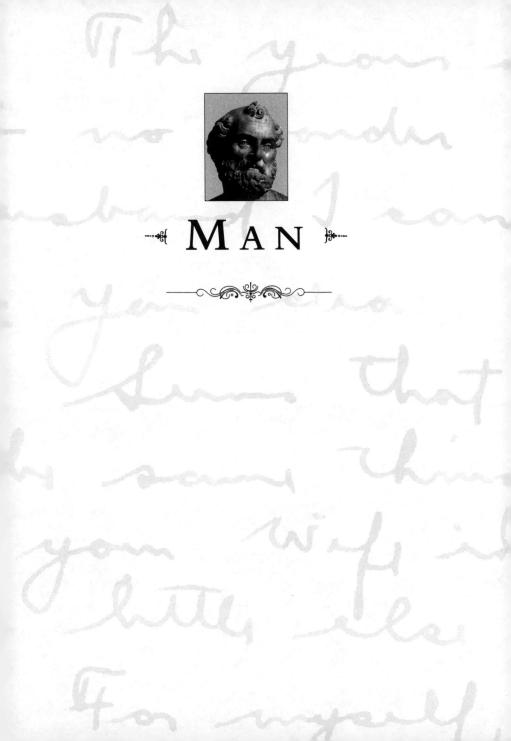

-◄ MAN ►-

CROSS-DRESSING, CLOTHES, MOTHER— SON AFFINITIES

VANESSA BELL TO HER SON

*a moustache was enough to make several people convinced
I was a man*

PIER PAOLO PASOLINI

one must forget, dear Fatty, one must forget them

MAURICE RAVEL

Still no letter!

ISAAC BABEL

I believe I wrote you that I'd found my galoshes

A. E. HOUSMAN

My gondolier expressed a wish that he were your son

ST.-JOHN PERSE

it is I, the man, who feel I am becoming a horse

Vanessa Bell *(1879–1961)*

to her son Quentin Bell

When Virginia Woolf's sister, British painter Vanessa Bell, donned a moustache and showed up at a gala with full skirts and facial hair, she was mistaken for a rather tall man in drag. This founding member of the sexually liberated Bloomsbury group lived apart from her husband, Clive Bell, and had a daughter by her live-in lover, the bisexual artist Duncan Grant, with whom she shared an enthusiasm for Postimpressionism. She found it amusing to see the world from the vantage point of a male being pursued by admirers of the same sex, and she shared this triumphant, rather dizzying view in a letter to her second son, Quentin.

June 22nd (1930)
8 Fitzroy Street, W. 1

My darling Quentin,

. . . I realised the other night what it must be like to be you! (footnote: i.e., a heterosexual male in a gay circle). We went to a party given by Eddy Sackville-West, one of those parties where the ladies dress as men, and vice versa. I put on a lovely male mask but otherwise was very female—or so I should have thought—wearing a crinoline and red silk coat and an Italian hat. However, such was the effect of the mask that the moment I entered the room I was seized on by E. Gathorne-Hardy (whom I had never met before) and who whirled me round in the dance and was so much intrigued he tried to get the mask off. I prevented him and managed to escape unscathed and unknown, but of course had to come down to my real female self later, as masks are too hot to wear for long. The odd thing was that a moustache was enough to make several people convinced I was a man. Never shall I have such a success again, I fear!

All women become like their mothers: that is their tragedy. No man does. That's his.

—Oscar Wilde

PIER PAOLO PASOLINI *(1922–1975)*

A posthumous find among the Italian film director's papers is a recurrent reverie he had when asked about his mother: they are alone, walking along a path, and it's springtime in Sacile, bushes are about to bud, mountains are visible beyond the black trunks of trees, which are still bare, and primroses are already in bloom—a scene he films in Mamma Roma. *"This gives me an infinite joy that, even now ... overwhelms me. I squeeze my mother's arm tightly (indeed we're walking arm in arm) and bury my cheek in the modest fur coat that she's wearing: in that fur coat I smell the odor of spring, a mixture of cold and warmth, of fragrant mud and of flowers still without fragrance, of house and countryside. This odor of my mother's modest fur coat is the odor of my life."*

[Postmark: Rome]
[7 October 1950]

My little darling,

I got your two rather sad postcards: the first, while it wrung my heart, made me smile a little at the thought of your culinary apprehensions; the second on the other hand would have distressed me had it not reached me on a morning of good news. Muscetta, secretary to Einaudi (the publisher and not the president, because you are capable of all kinds of interpretations!), wanted to meet me to ask me for my manuscript of Friulian poems: so a possible publication by Einaudi! Then there are other prospects which I shall write to you about when I am more certain. But I hope you will arrive here meantime; I have a terrible desire to see you again.

Meanwhile I shall tell you—I know these things interest you— that I have bought myself the material for a coat, very elegant, latest fashion, pure wool, all for 8500 lire, that is to say half price. It was a great bargain even according to Gigino and his wife. Aunt

Giannina had said that together with my father she would give me it this Christmas; so meantime I have used my money and then, if they can, they will let me have it back. So it is a saving as well.

There is no other immediate news. Don't worry about the flowers—do you think anyone will have forgotten that the 4th is his birthday? But the other things, the Germans, etc., one must forget, dear Fatty, one must forget them.

I kiss and hug you with infinite tenderness,

Yours, Pier Paolo

*D*ear Fatty" was but one of many pet names Pasolini had for her—no doubt all more mellifluous in Italian.

On the second postcard Pasolini refers to in his letter, his mother had written of Pier Paolo's brother (not her favorite):

"Today is Guido's birthday. I wonder if anyone will remember to go and take flowers! Do you remember how for his birthday he wanted me to make strudel with new apples and grapes? Do you remember how six years ago today you were in the steeple at Casarsa hiding because there were the Germans and round-ups of men? What terrible and sad days! And yet Guido was still with us and we were happy."

. . . Has the trunk reached Quincy St.? Pray guard jealously my few clothes—a summer suit and a coat, and two white waistcoats that I would give much for here, now. But don't let Father and Willy wear them out, as they will serve me still. Farewell, sweet mother. [. . .] Love abounding to all. [. . .]

Yours ever,

H.

—Henry James

MAURICE RAVEL *(1875–1937)*

Maurice Ravel's mother, a woman of Basque heritage, was the deepest emotional tie in his life, and the folksongs she sang him as a child were the source of his love for Spanish music. Madame Ravel's devotion was every bit as strong. When urged by a friend to convert to Catholicism, Marie Delouart Ravel declined, saying she would "prefer to be in hell with her family than in heaven all alone." The French composer probably inherited some of his musical sensibilities from his father, too, who as a child yearned to play the flute, but was told it would give him a stomachache. He settled for the trumpet instead. Here Ravel writes to his mother from the headquarters of the Thirteenth Artillery Regiment, where he served as an ambulance driver during World War I, when the sound of the siren was the music of the day.

March 26, 1916
Conducteur Ravel
Convoisautomobiles
Section T.M. 171
par B.C.M. Paris

Mama dearest,

Still no letter! It's already 18 days since I left Paris, and since that time only my friends have written to me. All of them, even those to whom I didn't write.

You know however that you don't have to write literature. Tell me what's new, what you are doing, the visits you receive, what is happening to Edouard. It's not that complicated; you have all the time to do it, and I won't be in this sad situation of a poilu without a family—but with a correspondent, because Madame Dreyfus has adopted me as her godson.

Love,
Maurice

*A*nother musician who had an instrument chosen for him was Elvis Presley, whose mother, Gladys, thought a bicycle was too dangerous for her only child, so she bought him a guitar instead. While she never stepped on his blue suede shoes, Gladys was close on the heels of her baby boy with a bulldog tenacity the Memphis Mafia couldn't match. The two were so close they shared a private language of babytalk, which he frantically prattled over her dead body during her funeral, lamenting, "My baby's gone!" Such filial devotion spilled onto the silver screen in his first film, *Love Me Tender*, in which he sang the title song not to a leading lady, but to his movie mother, Mildred Dunnock.

ISAAC BABEL *(1894–1941)*

With his mother and sister living in Belgium, his wife and daughter in Paris, Babel remained in Russia, except for several Paris sojourns, and, as his letters show, he struggled for both money to send his family and peace in which to write—not easily won, this peace, from either the world or himself. Every story went through numerous drafts (up to twenty-six) as Babel excised each unnecessary word, however beautiful. He often disappeared quite suddenly to be free of all disturbance—which left his friends with disappearance anecdotes to relate when he was rehabilitated and celebrated in 1964, after the Stalinist purges that took Babel as one much grieved and beloved victim—"with spectacles on [his] nose and autumn in [his] heart," as he described himself.

Moscow
October 13, 1926

Dear Mama,
Yesterday I attended to household chores. I sent the wash to the laundry (a crisis in underpants is threatening, because they are literally disintegrating). The cleaning woman has washed, scrubbed, steamed our room. We have so many bedbugs that it has become a

legend among the other dwellers in our apartment. Just imagine!

I believe I wrote you that I'd found my galoshes. I gave my shoes—the big ones—to be mended and it turned out that our shoemaker, Prakht, had died. A boil appeared on his neck—septicemia—and now a younger shoemaker sits on his bench. [. . .]

[. . .] Be well and toothy.

Yours,

Isya

*B*edbugs make an intoxicating appearance in one of Babel's Odessa stories: "Each commodity had a price of its own, and each sum was wetted down with Bessarabian wine, redolent of bedbugs." As for motherhood, in one of Babel's early Odessa stories, "Liubka the Cossack," the recently un-employed Tsudechkis winds up general manager of Liubka's inn-yard after showing this all-over-the-place entrepreneur how to wean her baby boy (with a comb's teeth protruding from her breast) as Tsudechkis and she become acquainted, hard on the heels of her maternal endearments: "I'm coming up to you right now, you little gangster,' Liubka muttered, apostrophizing her son, and dashed for the staircase. She came into the room and took her breast out of her dusty blouse."

A. E. HOUSMAN (1859–1936)

This letter announces both a favorite new backdrop and a favorite new character in Housman's life. The gondolier, Andrea, so charmingly introduced here, became one of the reasons for Housman's frequent visits to Venice over the next seven years, and even after he'd fallen out of love, he responded to Andrea's deathbed summons by traveling to see him, then regularly sending money to alleviate discomfort while the gondolier lingered on for another four years. In a poem of 1908, his vanished love for Andrea is cast in the image of a fallen belfry.

15 October 1990 17
North Road

My dear Mamma,

[...] Often at sunset I used to go up the great bell-tower in St. Mark's Place. Venice looks like one large island (the canals cannot be seen): the lagoon lies all round, [...] and the water declares its depth or shallowness by its colour: as the sun goes down it turns partly a golden green and partly a pale vermilion.

My gondolier expressed a wish that he were your son. He wanted me to come to Venice next Christmas, and I explained that at Christmas I went to see you; and then he made this remark. The reason is, that if he were your son he would be well off and would have no family to provide for: so at least he says. At present he has to earn a living for one wife, two sisters, one mother, one mother-in-law, and half an uncle (who was once a champion oarsman and is now paralysed); which is pretty good for a young man of twenty-three who has had one eye kicked out by a horse. [...]

Your loving son
A. E. Housman

St.-John Perse (1887–1975)

Born Alexis Léger on the coral island of Saint-Léger-les-Feuilles, near Guadeloupe, St.-John Perse, educated in France, became both a poet and diplomat; in the latter capacity he was sent to China, the locus of these letters. His long poems, of immense breath, sing the sense of man on earth, with its waters, winds, and place in the cosmos—a place that St.-John Perse said is understood only when the land recognizes its subservience to the sea, "woven in us, to the last weaving of its tangled night." The sea, the sound of his childhood, calls to him as he gallops across inland China.

Peking
April 4, 1917

Dearest Mother,

[. . .] I think of you a great deal; you are so much on my mind in the midst of all my work. [. . .]

The only thing I begin to miss in the immense space that seems to surround me is, immensely, the sea. And I have a strange sensation, which I seem to share with my horse when we stop in some remote spot on the Chinese plain—a sensation of being stirred by some sort of mysterious waves that cause us both instinctively to turn—at first, only our heads, but then the entire axis of our bodies—in unison in the direction of the sea, as my little pocket-compass confirms. I'm sure that you are familiar with the law of animal magnetism that is denied by our European scientists. But you probably never had a chance to feel its effect, as a horsewoman, because of your dislike for that old enemy of yours, the sea.

My Mongolian horse, a primitive beast, sometimes seems to be so completely one with me that it is I, the man, who feel I am becoming a horse, and that my horse considers me his totem—a strange and eerie impression, it seems so real. I think it goes back to my childhood.

Other than the sea and all it means to me spiritually, the only thing that is dangerously lacking for me here is music. [. . .] Do take care of yourself, dear Mother. You are always in my heart, and it is you who keep it from becoming too gloomy and empty at times.

Your son, A.

VAUNTING

JAMES ABBOTT McNEILL WHISTLER

It is a noble work, though, Mother, and one we may be proud of

PAUL CÉZANNE

I know that he has a good opinion of me who have a very good opinion of myself

T. S. ELIOT

I am now fully established as assistant editor of the Egoist

ERNEST HEMINGWAY

I do not care for this type of publicity and will not permit it

GEORGE SAND TO HER SON

Ho, ho, Mr. Mayor, you had better step carefully

TENNESSEE WILLIAMS

I have been finishing a new play (a comedy*!)*

ISAAC BABEL

I look like a cheerful pug

HENRI DE TOULOUSE-LAUTREC

I'm sweating like a bull and I kiss you

James Abbott McNeill Whistler *(1834–1903)*

Like the acclaimed peacocks he was so proud of painting for his patron Frederick Leyland's opulent London dining room, Whistler was fond of preening, even for his mother, who considered him the cock of the walk. This American painter, who lived in England and France most of his life, was a compulsive artist from a young age. In his youth, he seldom drew in his room, but on it, and his landlord, upon seeing the walls covered with his sketches, made a fuss when coming to collect the rent, which was (as usual) in arrears. "Now, now, never mind," Whistler assured him. "I'll not charge you anything for the decorations." Earlier in Paris, young Whistler mentioned his mother to a friend, who replied incredulously, "Your mother? Who would have thought of you having a mother, Jimmy?" "Yes, indeed, I have a mother," said the artist, "and a very pretty bit of color she is, I can tell you." Ironically, he would paint her a dozen years later in a work he titled Arrangement in Black and Gray: The Artist's Mother.*

Willie, referred to in this letter, is Whistler's brother; Princess Louise is Queen Victoria's sculptress daughter, who admired his work.

[Summer of 1876]

My Own Darling Mother,

I must not wait any longer that I may tell you what I have longed to do, the completion of this famous dining room. How I have worked. There must still be another week of it, or even two, before I can leave it, and say *I am content*. It is a *noble* work, though, Mother, and one we may be proud of, so very beautiful! and so entirely new, and original, as you can well fancy it would be, for at least *that* quality is recognized in your son.

Willie has told you of the visit of the Princess Louise to the "Peacock Palace," in Princes Gate, and her delight in the "gorgeous loveliness" of the work. Also the Marquis of Westminster . . . and everybody else. I know you will be pleased that this testimony of worth should be offered after so much labor, therefore I tell you. The mere visits of Princes, and Dukes, we well know is no *voucher* for the *quality* of a work of art, for they are simply curious people, generally better *mannered* than others about them, but able to look with the same satisfaction upon a *bad* thing, as a good one. Still they are *charming* people, and show *real* delight in this beautiful room, keep up the buzz of publicity most pleasantly in London society, and this is well, and I hope good may result.

I am tired, but well, I am happy to say. Good night, dearest Mother, it is late, and I must get to my work again tomorrow. [. . .]

Your loving son,
Jamie

PAUL CÉZANNE (1839–1906)

Paul Cézanne once painted his mother and sister playing the music of Tannhaüser (Wagner being a big influence in his earlier turbulent paintings), with his father, on the sofa, painted out. Behind her husband's back, Elizabeth Cézanne gave her son steady encouragement in whatever he wished to become. Although Madame Cézanne became more feisty with age, Paul cared for her until her death, telling her stories to keep her amused, taking her for drives, lifting her from the carriage and carrying her like a child in his arms to her chair. And all that in spite of the fact that Cézanne couldn't bear to be touched unexpectedly and would fly into a fury if a servant's sleeve or skirt brushed against him at table. He was not quite so sensitive to art critics and the opinion of the public, who never gave him pause as he went his own way, helping create the revolutionary changes in the art of this century.

Paris
26th September, 1874

My dear Mother,

In the first place let me thank you very much for thinking of me. For some days the weather has been beastly and very cold, but I am not ailing in any way and I make a good fire. [. . .]

Pisarro has not been in Paris for about a month and a half; he is in Brittany, but I know that he has a good opinion of me who have a very good opinion of myself. I am beginning to consider myself stronger than all those around me, and you know that the good opinion I have of myself has only been reached after mature consideration. I have still got to work, not so as to be able to add the final polish, which is for the admiration of imbeciles. And the thing that is commonly so much appreciated is merely the reality of the handwork and renders all work resulting from it inartistic and common. I must strive after perfection only for the pleasure of giving added truth and learning. And believe me, the hour always comes when one makes an impression and one has admirers far more fervent and convinced than those who are flattered by the empty appearances.

It is a very bad time for selling, all the bourgeois are unwilling to spend their sous, but this will end. . . .

My dear Mother, remember me to my sisters. [. . .]

Ever your son,
Paul Cézanne.

T. S. ELIOT *(1888–1965)*

T. S. Eliot, high priest of twentieth-century poetry and editor of the ground-breaking literary review the Egoist, *was an American who spent his prolific, influential years in England, an absence that occasioned a steady flow of letters to his mother. Until he was rescued by publishers Faber and Faber, which gave him further opportunity to bring out avant-garde literature, Eliot worked at a bank, where he snatched moments from the money to expand his repertoire of languages.*

Sunday 20 May 1917
18 Crawford Mansions

My dearest Mother,

[. . .] I am going to have a sort of promotion tomorrow—whether it will bring any immediate rise of salary I don't know. [. . .] The work during the day is rather irregular—often for an hour or more in the morning there is nothing to do at all, and I pull out a Spanish grammar which I keep by me and study away at that (when I get to read Spanish easily I think I will take up Danish or Portuguese). [...]

Another article of mine came out in the *New Statesman* on Saturday. [...] I am now fully established as assistant editor of the *Egoist*. I will send you the June issue when it comes out, though I don't know whether it will have anything of mine in it or not. My colleagues are a Miss Weaver, a funny little spinster, but quite nice, and I believe quite intelligent, and a Mrs. Aldington, better known as "H. D.", a poetess, who like most, or a good half of the world of art and letters in London, is an American. I went to see her this afternoon for the first time, and found her very agreeable and disposed to look upon me, for some reason, as a great authority upon Greek language and literature. London is an amazing place— one is constantly discovering new quarters; this woman lives in a most beautiful dilapidated old square [Mecklenburgh], which I had never heard of before; a square in the middle of town, near King's Cross Station, but with spacious old gardens about it. [...]

Always with very much love

Your devoted son

Tom

My beard is coming along fine. Makes me look sort of distinguished, like someone you'd care to know.

—William Faulkner, from Paris

ERNEST HEMINGWAY (1899–1961)

Gertrude Stein, the Big Mama of the Lost Generation, taught Hemingway a new rhythm while bouncing him on her knee and encouraging him to cut out the adjectives. The American author—an institution unto himself with such classics as For Whom the Bell Tolls *and* The Sun Also Rises*—suffered a more traumatic relationship with his real mother, however. His liaison with this first woman in his life became turbulent when she dressed him as a toddler in girl's clothes so he and his older sister Marcelline might go out in public as twins. But sometimes Grace Hemingway, a staunch Christian woman zealous about presenting matching kiddies to the world, would dress them as little boys, and then it was Marcelline's turn to take a gender beating. One thing Grace couldn't do was stop Marcelline from growing taller than Ernest, short of cutting off her legs. And in this letter he threatens to cut his mother off financially if she were to talk to magazine editors longing for the lowdown on his babyhood.*

. . . Scribner's have written me that some woman from McCalls magazine, I believe, was contacting them to get in touch with you to write a piece about me when I was a boy. I do not care for this type of publicity and will not permit it. I told Scribners to write the woman, who was a very pushing, and vicious and, I thought, rather a detestable type of journalist, that I contributed to your support and that I would withdraw this contribution in case they published any such article without my consent. Hope this handled that matter.

G E O R G E   S A N D   *(1804–1876)*

TO HER SON, MAURICE DUDEVANT

Best-selling French novelist George Sand (Amandine-Aurore-Lucile Dudevant), with her cigars and trousers, gave birth to a son and daughter. But her biggest baby was Chopin, whom she nursed to health when she wasn't lounging under the fragile composer's piano, nursing her muse. Sand lived high drama, even as she confronted death. When the family tomb was opened to receive the newly deceased body of her beloved grandmother, the old family tutor, Deschartes, unearthed the remains of her father and requested that she kiss his head, which had become detached from his skeleton. In a state of exaltation, Sand did. In love with revolution, she dabbled ardently in politics, which the following letter supports. Here in a giddy state, she playfully lords it over her son, Maurice, who was mayor of Nohant, reminding him that mother— particularly one dressed in pants—knows best.

March 24th, 1848:

Here I am, already doing a stateman's work. I have drawn up two government circulars today, one for the Ministry of Public Instruction, the other for the Ministry of the Interior. It amuses me to think that they will go out addressed to *'All Mayors,'* and that you will be receiving through official channels your *mother's* instructions! Ho, ho, Mr. Mayor, you had better step carefully, and begin by reading out each Sunday one of the Bulletins of the Republic to your assembled National Guard. . . . I do not know whether I am standing on my head or my heels. There is somebody at me all the time. But this kind of life suits me. . . .

TENNESSEE WILLIAMS *(1 9 1 1 – 1 9 8 3)*

Edwina Dakin Williams was a Southern belle who, like Amanda Wingfield in her son's brilliant play, The Glass Menagerie, *dreamed of bygone days of cotillions and gentlemen callers, but she put her foot down when it came to committing her son Tom (Tennessee to the rest of us) to a mental hospital during a serious bout with drugs. He then described her as a little Prussian officer in drag, but was also devoted to her, flying her out to attend his opening nights and keeping her well stocked with letters (in this one, a play,* Period of Adjustment, *is born, and a pet pooch nearly dies). His remarkable ability to write strong, true roles for women—some of the best in American theater— surely evolved in part from Edwina's delicate yet cast-iron character.*

Dear Mother:

I have been finishing a new play (a *comedy!*) which I am going to try out at the Coconut Grove Playhouse with an all-Broadway cast. We start rehearsals December 18th and open the 29th and I'm going to direct it myself so this month is going to be pretty lively for me. I do hope you will fly down here for Xmas. And see the opening. Everyone seems to feel it will be a happy event and our cast is wonderful: Barbara Baxley who played the gypsy's daughter in "Camino Real," Cliff Robertson who played the male lead in "Orpheus Descending," and three other first-rate players. [. . .]

Miss Brinda had another heat-stroke in Key West, it was terribly hot there, but she survived it again. She had the remarkable sense to jump into the bath-tub and stand there under the faucet. I mean lie under it, as she was just about "out." The faucet was dripping and the veterinary says this probably saved her life, as no one was in the house with her at the time. She had a 106 fever, received penicillin to prevent pneumonia and was rubbed with ice till she got back on her bow-legs, and is now as well as usual.—Key West is too hot for her. So was Rome last summer. The poor thing leads a dog's life!

Wire or call me collect soon as you've made your plans about Xmas. I want you to be my guest here.

Much love,

Tom

ISAAC BABEL (*1894–1941*)

It was in quite a different material that Babel found himself wrapped upon the publication of Articles and Materials, *noted in this letter, which included Babel's autobiography and several critical essays on the Odessa writer and his short stories, of which "My First Goose" was one. Although we read here a straightforward reckoning of money en route to his mother, his messages about such matters were often mysterious. If he wanted to say he was sending fifty francs from Paris, he would pretend to be writing of books and say "The first volume will be small—only fifty pages." He had to change lodgings at one point in Paris because the madwoman from whom he was renting thought he was a bandit, was frightened of him, and said she'd have him locked up.*

Paris

May 21, 1928

Mother!

I've sent you one hundred *belgas* today. They've given Zhenya an appointment at the Ministry about your French visas. [. . .]

A collection of articles about me has just come out in Russia. It makes very amusing reading—quite incomprehensible. It was written by frightfully scholarly fools. Reading it, I get the impression that I'm reading about a dead man—what I am doing

now is so different from what I did before. The book is adorned
with my portrait by Altman and it's quite funny too—I look like a
cheerful pug. I'll send you the collection tomorrow. Please don't
lose it—I must, after all, make a collection of that sort of thing. I
haven't done a thing for three days. I had put too much pressure
upon my brains and got overtired. Now I seem to have recovered
and tomorrow again, *je me remets au travail.* [. . .]

I have read that you're having glorious weather in Brussels,
while here it is raining, *mes amis,* raining every day, in every form—
downpours, fine drizzles through a heavenly sieve, and on Sundays,
to mark the holidays, rain mixed with hail. And this is called *la douce
France* and *Ville Lumière.* Ah, give me Odessa any time.

. . . And on that note, my lovelies, period and until tomorrow.

Yours,

I.

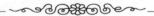

"The evening wrapped me in its dusky sheets of
revivifying moisture and laid a maternal palm on
my burning forehead."

—Isaac Babel, "My First Goose"

Henri de Toulouse-Lautrec *(1864–1901)*

Caught up in a flurry of activity and enjoying to the full his recognition as an artist during this productive time in his life, Toulouse-Lautrec sends a breezy letter to his maman, *typical of his almost daily messages. The book he mentions on the Jews was* Au Pied de Sinai, *for which he supplied thirteen lithograph illustrations. As for the forgiveness Henri mentions, he had reason to ask her pardon:* Maman Toulouse-Lautrec, *although she gave herself to her boy and did all she could do to further his artistic development, did keep a tight fist on her* francs *and* sous, *in every household transaction and distribution. She wore her clothes till they gave out on her, whereupon she sold them—but her letter-writing shows intrepid innovation in making "petites économies." Having filled four pages of a folded letter sheet, she spun it around ninety degrees and carried on across the already fully covered paper, creating quite a scrawled sight to behold and decipher.*

[Paris]

[May 1897]

My dear Mama,

Terrible heat, which hit us all of a sudden. I'm winding everything up and am going to face the move, or rather moves . [...]

My friend Joyant has definitely bought the Goupil gallery. I'm finishing a book with Clemenceau on the Jews. My publisher owes me 1,200 francs. He'll give me 300 of it tomorrow. Let me know if you can advance me 500 francs on the 900 balance. Repayable in six months. If you can't, I'll make other arrangements. I hope to place my maid in a good house. I'm sweating like a bull and I kiss you.

Your boy,

Henri

Forgive all the figures, but business is business [...]

P.S. I'm thinking of painting a portrait of a friend of mine at Mal-
romé. I've naturally invited the model himself, M. Paul LeClercq.
A young man of the world and of the best. This way you'll have
the pleasure of my company. I shall go first to Burgundy.

Yours,

H.

TRAVELOGUE

JOHANN WOLFGANG VON GOETHE

Farewell and love me

WILLIAM RANDOLPH HEARST

The total eclipse was over. [. . .] I had dropped out of the skies back on earth again

ST.-JOHN PERSE

My chest is still expanding, at my age

A. E. HOUSMAN

The cathedral is quite a failure, high-shouldered and almost mean-looking

HENRY JAMES

I have retired from the glittering scene [. . .] to commune with my mammy

T. S. ELIOT

gorgeous southern shrubs, and warm smells of garlic— donkeys—ox carts

J O H A N N   W O L F G A N G   V O N   G O E T H E   *(1 7 4 9 – 1 8 3 2)*

Goethe, Europe's colossus of a writer who took on both heaven and hell, was reborn—creatively, that is—when he toured Italy in 1786. It was a rebirth for which his mother must have served as midwife, intimately sharing his travels and travails through letters. When the German author of The Sorrows of Young Werther *and* Faust *passed through towns incognito, sometimes she might have been the only one who knew where he was. Here, their meeting practically sounds like a lover's tryst. Catherina Goethe had her son when she was just eighteen, later explaining their closeness by saying, "We were young together." Invited to a party on the day of her death, she declined, saying that Madam Goethe could not come as she was engaged just then in dying.*

[To Frau CATHARINA ELISABETH GOETHE]

Rome,

4th November 1786.

First I must tell you, my dear Mother, that I have reached here happy and well. I very much enjoyed the journey which I made quite secretly. I came through Bavaria and the Tyrol, and by Verona, Vicenza, Padua, Venice, Ferrara, Bologna, and Florence. I travelled quite alone and unknown and I am keeping up a kind of incognito here, too.

I can't tell you how happy it makes me to find so many of my life's dreams and wishes unravelled, to see in reality things that I have seen from childhood prints, things Father so often talked about.

[. . .] I don't know yet how long I shall stay; it will depend on how things go on at home. In any case, I'll return through Switzerland and come to you. And we shall have a grand time together; but we'll keep that a secret between us two. [. . .]

Write soon all about how things are with you, and any other news; abroad, any news of friends and dear ones is of interest. Tell me too when this letter reaches you, to give me an idea.

Farewell and love me.

WILLIAM RANDOLPH HEARST *(1863–1951)*

Phoebe Hearst, a formidable philanthropist and remarkable woman with a passion for architecture all her own, rarely joined her son, William, in his travels after his marriage, although he frequently invited her. As she refused just as frequently, he regaled her with picturesque letters like this one following an eclipse in Spain during his honeymoon with Millicent.

The Spanish faces got more worried than ever for with the darkness and the wind and rain and the uncanny cold it did kind of look as if the end of things might be at hand and a Spaniard must hate to go to judgment. . . .

All of a sudden it was gone and then there was a second or so before we realized the mystery and the beauty of the spectacle. . . .

There seemed to be a wonderful calm and peace and we really appeared to be transported away from the earth and to be in the presence of the machinery of the universe. . . .

The total eclipse was over. I was sorry. I had dropped out of the skies back on earth again.

I had come back from my strange world to the one that I was familiar with—and not to the most attractive part of it either. . . . [. . .]

S T . - J O H N P E R S E *(1887–1975)*

When St.-John Perse accepted the Nobel Prize for Literature in Stockholm in 1960, he spoke of the poet's purpose to consecrate the alliance between man and the creation, of the land as the vassal of the sea, which his rides in China recalled to him, as he and his beloved horse Allan turned to face the sea. In his poem "Praises" he sings of these interconnections among the human, the animal, and the divine:

"I loved a horse—who was he?—and sometimes (for animals know better the forces that praise us)
Snorting, he would lift to his gods a head of bronze, covered with a petiole of veins."

Peking
February 2, 1918

Dearest Mother,

[. . .] My horseback outings do me a world of good, physically and morally. My chest is still expanding, at my age, so much so that I can't button the first button of my sports jacket. By now Allan and I are complete friends; he is as accustomed to my voice as to that of a close friend. I've become very attached to this wild animal whose twitching ear always seems to expect an intelligible word from me. [. . .]

At first, like any self-respecting Central Asiatic horse, Allan couldn't abide the smell of foreigners; and even after he had established magnetic contact with me, looking me straight in the eye and quivering at the touch of my hand on his neck, he still seemed bothered by the smell of my Scotch tweeds. He now comes up to me with childlike eyes, oblivious of his ugliness and lack of manners. He comes right into the house, slipping around on the tile floor of the reception room, though I have to be careful to cover up a mirror that terrifies him. [...]

A. E. HOUSMAN *(1859–1936)*

By the light of a solitary candle, Housman, immersed in the Mediterranean, paints detailed pictures of Italian architecture awash in blinding sunlight or gentle moonlight. He even describes one cathedral in Pisa with unsettling human characteristics.

13 September 1901
[Castelfranco]

My dear Mamma,

This is written in pouring rain at the town of Castelfranco, which most likely you never heard of, and no more did I till four or five days ago. The pen and ink are too awful, so I must go on in pencil, which is all the better as there is no blotting paper. This is about twenty miles inland from Venice: it is celebrated as the birthplace of Giorgione, and as containing the only picture which is known with certainty to be his. [...] I have been at Paris, Pisa and Florence, and now lastly at Venice. Pisa is a rather handsome and very sleepy town, with all its chief buildings, the Cathedral, Baptistery and leaning tower, packed in one corner on an open space of grass, surrounded on two sides by the ancient walls of the city, which still run right round it. The weather was very hot and bright, and by daytime one could hardly open one's eyes to look at things; for although the Cathedral etc. are about as old as any Norman

architecture that we have got in England, they are chiefly built of
Carrara marble, which in process of time does indeed become
smeary and untidy, but never becomes mellow and venerable; and
under an Italian sun it blazes like a dusty highroad. The cathedral is
quite a failure, high-shouldered and almost mean-looking outside,
handsome and roomy inside, but not a bit religious: bands of black
marble on white, looking painfully spick and span, in spite of its
antiquity. [. . .] By daylight the Baptistery is much the finest of the
group of buildings, but in twilight and moonlight I think the leaning
tower is superior, with its six rows of pillars picked out in light and
shade. [. . .] The Arno at Pisa, being penned within embankments,
is a respectable stream by moonlight, when you cannot see that it is
liquid mud: however, after all it is not so bad as the Exe at Exeter:
the Arno is like pea-soup, but the Exe is like tomato-soup. Between
Pisa and Florence the Arno at present is merely a shallow brook
meandering along a wide bed of pebbles: at Florence they try to
make it look decent by a series of dams, but in this dry summer it
does not succeed. I have only one candle, which is bothering my
eyes, and Florence would take up more space than I could fill before
I go to bed, so here I will stop, and try to address the envelope legibly
with the abandoned pen and ink.

Your loving son
A. E. HOUSMAN

HENRY JAMES *(1843–1916)*

In the fall of 1875, Henry James returned to Europe with the intention of living there, and after spending much of that year in Paris, where he got to know Turgenev and Flaubert, he felt England calling to him. Soon he was tucked into lodgings near Piccadilly Circus in London, "glittering, charming, civilised Paris" slipping away as a rougher town took him in. Ever the well-bred, genial, even deferent guest, he could retire to his room and indulge in more candid reactions. His letters were often his only outlet, although his fiction would also become the home of such portraits and observations. By the time he wrote this letter, James had finally had enough of Europe, which had claimed his affections and affinities since his childhood.

> Mentmore, Leighton Buzzard
> November 28th, 1880.

Dearest mammy,

   ...This is a pleasant Sunday, and I have been spending it [...] in a very pleasant place. 'Pleasant' is indeed rather an odd term to apply to this gorgeous residence, and the manner of life which prevails in it [...] Lady Rosebery (it is her enviable dwelling) asked me down here a week ago, and I stop till tomorrow a.m. [...] The house is a huge modern palace, filled with wonderful objects accumulated by the late Sir Meyer de Rothschild, Lady R.'s father. All of them are precious and many are exquisite, and their general Rothschildish splendour is only equalled by their profusion.

   [...] They are at afternoon tea downstairs in a vast, gorgeous hall, where an upper gallery looks down like the colonnade in Paul Veronese's pictures, and the chairs are all golden thrones, belonging to ancient Doges of Venice. I have retired from the glittering scene, to meditate by my bedroom fire on the fleeting character of earthly possessions, and to commune with my mammy, until a supreme being in the shape of a dumb footman arrives, to ventilate my shirt and turn my stockings inside out (the beautiful red ones imparted by Alice—which he must admire so much, though he doesn't venture to show it,) preparatory to my dressing for dinner. Tomorrow I return to London and to my personal occupation, always doubly valued after 48 hours passed among *ces gens-ci,* whose chief effect upon me is to sharpen my desire to distinguish myself by personal achievement, of however limited a character. It is the only answer one can make to their atrocious good fortune. Lord Rosebery, however, with youth, cleverness, a delightful face, a happy character, a Rothschild wife of numberless millions to distinguish and demoralize him, wears them with such tact and bonhomie that you almost forgive him. [. . .]

Ever your fondest

H. JAMES jr.

T. S. ELIOT *(1888–1965)*

In London, Eliot would sometimes wear pale green powder to intensify his poetic pallor (not at the bank, surely, but in his other persona as high priest of modern literature through his editorship of the Egoist *and as author of* Four Quartets, The Waste Land, The Cocktail Party, *and* Murder in the Cathedral*). Here we find him on holiday with Vivien in a more colorful tableau. Eliot the sensualist swoons in southern France, his letter breaking off as he enters the garden: the heady fragrances and* joie de vivre *seduce him away from pen and paper, the sun of the Midi suffusing his mood and no doubt retinting his complexion.*

14 October 1919

—Perigueux is a town that I like. The last time I was there was at Christmas (1910), and arriving early on an intensely hot August morning it seemed more southern than it had before. It is a small old town, the metropolis of that district. It had taken me thirty-six hours to get there, but I felt that I had left London—the London of four years of war—and reached the South at one instant— suddenly Roman ruins, and tall white houses, and gorgeous southern shrubs, and warm smells of garlic—donkeys—ox carts. There is a particular excitement about arriving at an exciting place after a sleepless night of travel. We went to the hotel which had that musty smell I have only found in France and Italy, and I fell straight asleep on a bed, only waking for lunch. I stuffed myself with the good French food, which is as good and plentiful as ever, but more expensive. Then we sat out in a garden [Unfinished]

FESTIVITIES AND OUTINGS

ST.-JOHN PERSE

My dear old Minister, who is crazy about the theater, runs about on the stage during rehearsals with his glasses pushed up on his forehead, brandishing his stage-manager's cane

HENRI DE TOULOUSE-LAUTREC

I thank you for the prospective truffles

WILLIAM MAKEPEACE THACKERAY

Well, let us both be thankful that those eels have such an admirable brown sauce and that the champagne is iced to a nicety

WILLIAM RANDOLPH HEARST

Then he kissed Millie quite a smack and patted her on the head

T. S. ELIOT

Tonight it is raining torrents, which rejoices me

JOHANN WOLFGANG VON GOETHE'S MOTHER

The people who sit near and about me had better not so much as blow their noses

St.-John Perse *(1887–1975)*

In an earlier letter to his mother from China, St.-John Perse had written of his developing camaraderie with Alexandre Conty, a French diplomat in Peking, "not to mention the patience with which, in the evening under the lamplight, I have to listen to him read his favorite plays. (He is haunted by the theater, and he secretly hankers for it—the true calling that he missed.)" Successfully avoiding the stage on this occasion, the French diplomat and poet would later find himself on the world stage as the Nobel laureate for his poetry in 1960.

Peking
May 25, 1917

Dearest Mother,

[. . .] I've been swamped here this past week with the organizing of a big official celebration in the Legation gardens [. . .] a theater to be constructed to accommodate six hundred persons, a comic opera to be put on complete with orchestra and chorus, stars and supers—all this with only amateurs to draw on and train. My dear old Minister, who is crazy about the theater, runs about on the stage during rehearsals with his glasses pushed up on his forehead, brandishing his stage-manager's cane. He's never had such a good time. It breaks your heart to think he doesn't dare act in the play himself because the audience may include the very highest Chinese dignitaries. For myself, naturally, I was able to plead all the work at the Legation to avoid once and for all having to make a stage appearance.

HENRI DE TOULOUSE-LAUTREC *(1864–1901)*

Purveyors of vice in Montmartre kept Toulouse-Lautrec in alcohol and other debaucheries, and his doctor's brother could usually be counted on for main dishes with wings. But Henri turned to his chère Maman *in the Midi for seasonal and regional specialties.*

[Paris]

[December 1891]

My dear Mama,

I begin by reassuring you about Papa's condition, he had a touch of influenza and treated it at the Turkish bath. The steam room suffocated him and after a brief fainting spell he was quickly up on his feet thanks to a few glasses of kümmel. He's still watching himself but looks well enough.

[…] I thank you for the prospective truffles. If you send me a fowl stuffed with truffles, write on the address the weight:

Fowl so much

Truffles so much

because the excise charges are exorbitant when this precaution isn't taken.

Another thing. Towards the end of next week and towards the end of the one after have a fowl—capon or chicken—sent to me. Bourges' brother, who usually supplies the poultry, is off on a two-week trip.

Has the goose-liver season started? If it has, remember to have a dozen tins sent to me. I am re-reading my letter and find it to have a gastronomic character. My poster is pasted today on the walls of Paris and I'm going to do another one.

Affectionate regards to everyone around you whom it may concern.

I kiss you.

Yours,

Henri

WILLIAM MAKEPEACE THACKERAY *(1811–1863)*

Unlike his fellow Victorian writer George Eliot, Thackeray did not call his novels his children. Instead, he took on the various personae of his characters, signing his letters throughout his life with the names of people in his novels — Michael Angelo Titmarsh or Arthur Pendennis. He once described to his mother one of his fictitious heroes as having a "handsome likeness of an ugly son of yours." The satirical writer experienced an intense relationship with his mother, Anne, who loved him with a fierce possessiveness, but sent him from India to England on his own at age five and a half. His ensuing time spent in a Southampton boarding school was so awful that he later wrote, "I remember kneeling by my little bed of a night, and saying, 'Pray God, I may dream of my mother!'" As an adult, Thackeray reacted to her religious excesses with a hearty enjoyment of his own worldly excesses — gambling, cigars, champagne, and good food — which he pays homage to in this letter.

ST. JAMES'S STREET

1844

MY DEAREST MAMMY,—Your letter of Saturday arrived here on Wednesday morning—does n't it seem impudent to say I have had no time to answer it till now?—but somehow the day has passed and the postman's bell stopped ringing and it was n't done. What a picture you give of the place—Paris! I wish September were come. I will come then, please God, for ten days [. . .] I wish you had never come, that's the truth—for I fancied myself perfectly happy until then—now I see the difference: and what a deal of the best sort of happiness it is God's will that I should lose. Whitebait dinners are all very well, but—hang the buts—it is those we are always sighing after. Well, let us both be thankful that those eels have such an admirable brown sauce and that the champagne is iced to a nicety: a man can't have everything. There is no fun in writing this, though—the paper gets dim before my eyes and it is the scene of parting all over again. Don't fancy that I'm unhappy, though; it's only the abstract pathos of the thing that moves me. I never could bear to think of children parted from their parents somehow without a tendency to blubbering; and am as weak to this day upon the point, as I used to be at School. In the meanwhile it will be a consolation to you to know this tender-hearted being is cruelly hungry, and in twenty minutes from this time will be on his way to a jollification. God bless all.

W. M. T.

WILLIAM RANDOLPH HEARST (1863–1951)

Phoebe Hearst did not attend her son Will's lavish wedding, at New York's Grace Church, claiming illness and remaining at her hacienda. She sent her daughter-in-law a magnificent brooch of emeralds—which the groom said was the "climax of the day," although it was also quite climactic that he so defied his mother's wishes in this marriage. After the honeymoon party arrived in Paris, Hearst wrote his mother a jaunty, amusing description of the wedding she'd missed, and the big splash the brooch had made on board.

Hotel Wagram, 208, Rue de Rivoli
Paris
May, 1903

[. . .] The chantry was very beautifully decorated with colored roses and apple blossoms. Our wedding was cheerful and not to be mistaken for a funeral. Some thirty of our friends were present.

[. . .] The bishop looked very grand and solemn. Anita came up with Millie and her pa. They didn't have any bouquet. I had forgotten to bring it. Millie didn't mind. She stepped up alongside me trembling and frightened. The bishop married us. Then he kissed Millie quite a smack and patted her on the head and told her he wanted her to come and see him when she returned and that she and he would "keep tabs" on me. Then I kissed Millie and the audience <u>applauded</u>. The bishop hushed them and appeared to be rather shocked but wasn't. [. . .]

After the marriage a few of us went to the Waldorf. We had not intended to have a wedding breakfast but we had to have some kind of breakfast as not many had eaten anything yet. [. . .]

Presents and reporters arrived alternately. I went down stairs and sent you a long telegram. I <u>hope</u> you got <u>that</u>. Then Millie and I went up stairs to Falk and got photographed to please the reporters. When we got back everybody had been drinking toasts and were in the usual wedding breakfast condition. We had had bouillon and now had ice cream. I don't know what happened between. It didn't happen to us.

Now it was three o'clock and time to go to the steamer. We drove to the docks. [. . .] We got aboard the boat and somebody pelted us with rice. . . . People began to suspect they had a bride on board. Then Benny brought your beautiful Brooch. It staggered <u>me</u> and Millie was just knocked all of a heap. She didn't know whether to laugh or cry. She had presence of mind enough to pin it on. She said she only wished she could have been married in it. Orrin said Mrs. Spreckels was on board. Millie said she didn't care, she guessed Mrs. Spreckels didn't have an emerald brooch like <u>that</u>. I sort of surmised she didn't either from the way she stared at it at dinner later. . . .

T. S. ELIOT *(1888–1965)*

Here the poet of "The Hollow Men" fills in unexpressed emotions and steps into a bucolic idyll, a hollow in the hills.

The Egoist, Oakley House
Bloomsbury Street, London, W.C.
24 October 1917

My dearest Mother,

I just wanted to write you a line as I did not by the last mail, though it is now late. I was very glad to get your letter and father's this morning, and to have a little news. You made me reflect that I am most often very inexpressive in my letters. But I am constantly thinking of you and picturing you in past scenes, and trying to picture me in the present. There are so many things I don't like to think of, because I think often that I used to be very selfish and self-indulgent in many ways, and quite unappreciative of your and father's kindness and generosity. [. . .]

We spent last Sunday in a most delightful farm, hidden away in the Surrey hills, about an hour and a half from town. There is a very nice farmer and his wife who do not take lodgers regularly, but they had formerly been gardeners to Lord Russell and to the Trevelyans, and so they took us in. The farm is in a little hollow in the hills, very high, surrounded by a ring of pine woods, broken only by a little narrow yellow winding road that wanders down into the valley. It is four miles from a village, completely in a forest; but you can walk about two miles and emerge suddenly on the top of Leith Hill, precipitous on the other side, with a view wide over the downs of Surrey and Sussex. We had beautiful weather too. I took down books and prepared my lecture on William Morris. I no longer *write* them—I set down about three pages of notes. Vivien says I am getting better and better as a lecturer.

Tonight it is raining torrents, which rejoices me. I must go to bed now.

with Very much love
your devoted son
Tom

JOHANN WOLFGANG VON GOETHE *(1749–1832)*

FROM HIS MOTHER, ELISABETH GOETHE

These tender excerpts illustrate the intimacy and wry humor Goethe's mother shared with her son. It's no small order, being the mother of a literary giant, but Frau Goethe comes across as unassuming and down-to-earth, giving credit where she feels credit is due, and showing herself to be a serious theatergoer and a fan of yet another influential German writer, Schiller.

November 30, 1804

... There is nothing else my heart desires, except that when you come upon something really beautiful to read, you will think of me. On New Year's Day Schiller's *Tell* will be performed in our theatre. So think of me that evening at 6 o'clock. The people who sit near and about me had better not so much as blow their noses. They can do that at home.

October 8, 1807

... The Fair this year was rich—in professors!!! Since a great part of your fame and repute falls like a cloak upon me, and since people imagine that I have contributed to your great talent—well, so they come gawp at me and I, I do not hide my light under a bushel but set it on a candlestick and tell the people that I did not make the slightest contribution to your greatness as a man and a poet (for who would accept undeserved praise?), but I do know very well to whom praise and thanks are due, seeing that in the germ in a mother's womb all that is you already existed without any help from me.

DEPARTURES

CHARLES BAUDELAIRE

You were both my idol and my comrade

GEORGE BERNARD SHAW

Do not spend too much on interviews with Oscar Wilde

JAMES BOSWELL

Mother gone. Was quite stupefied

MARC CHAGALL

Lighter than a flame, than an airy shadow, I hasten to shed tears

Charles Baudelaire *(1821–1867)*

In this excerpt from one of his later letters to his mother, Baudelaire gives himself over to a reverie of the halcyon days of his childhood—between the death of his own elderly father and his mother's marriage to Monsieur Aupick. Aupick became the bane of the poet's life, partly because from his arrival forward, Charles no longer possessed his mother totally, as he does in this recollection.

May 6, 1861

Dear mother,

. . . In my childhood there was a period when I loved you passionately; don't be afraid, listen and read. I never told you. I remember a cab ride; you were coming out of a nursing home where you had been staying, and you showed me, to prove that you had been thinking of your son, some pen and ink drawings you had done for me. Do I not have a remarkable memory? Later, there was Place St. André des Arts and Neuilly. . . . Long walks, continual endearments! I remember the quays which were so melancholy in the evening. For me those were the good days of maternal tenderness. I'm sorry to call "the good days" a time which was doubtless bad for you. But I was still alive for you; you were all mine. You were both my idol and my comrade. You may be surprised to find me talking with passion of such a remote past. I too am surprised. Perhaps it is because once again I want to die, that the old days seem so clear to the mind's eye.

*A*s Baudelaire reflects on his aging appearance in the following note, we are reminded of how his sense of women was related to furs, jewels, satin, the sounds and smells of femininity, and how he saw therein even the beginnings of his own vanity ("I loved my mother for her elegance . . . I was a precocious dandy."):

We haven't seen each other for fifteen months, and my hair is all grey, to the point that I am thinking of powdering it white. Don't laugh at the vanities of an old man.

After his mother's death, Flaubert used to get his house-keeper to dress up in her old check dress and surprise him with an apocryphal reality. It worked, and it didn't work: seven years after the funeral he would still burst into tears at the sight of that old dress moving about the house.

—**Julian Barnes,** *Flaubert's Parrot*

George Bernard Shaw *(1856–1950)*

A word is required—from the Beyond!—for the nature of this cryptic message to be divined, from one of Ireland's great playwrights to his mother concerning another of that country's stellar wags and dramaturges, Oscar Wilde. Shaw's mother, an occultist of long standing, and long sitting as well, held weekly séances each Friday in her London home. Note that this letter was written two years after Oscar Wilde died, saying, "My wallpaper and I are fighting a duel to the death. One or the other of us has to go." Curiously, Mrs. Shaw also dabbled in spirit drawings, which often resembled designs for wallpaper.

Victoria Hotel. Holkham

25 July 1902

My address for the present is as above. Do not spend too much on interviews with Oscar Wilde; and do not ask any questions that you know the answer to, as a reply would have no weight, unless indeed it were a wrong reply. And do not tell anybody else about the questions until you get them finally answered and hear from me as to what they mean.

GBS

Since Shaw was so intent on keeping these exchanges with the ex-Oscar, or next-Oscar, exclusively between his mother and himself, one wonders if the dearly departed wit and wag was ghostwriting some of Shaw's snappier lines.

JAMES BOSWELL *(1740–1795)*

The year 1766 found James Boswell, sidekick and biographer of Samuel Johnson, in Paris, when he received news from his father of his mother's death, as he records in his diary:

Tuesday 28 January. [. . .] Mother gone. Was quite stupefied. In all morning. Wept in bursts; prayed to her like most solemn Catholic to saint. Roused philosophy; sung Italian gently to soothe. [. . .] Had strong enthusiasm to comfort Father all his life.

Wednesday 29 January. Yesterday felt more the sad news. Recalled her kind, affectionate concern. Was deeply touched, but thinking of her being in heaven, was easy. Was pious and had manly hope. [. . .]

Friday 31 January. Yesterday morning after having been up all night [. . .] then was still in confusion. Cried, "Is it possible that my mother is dead?" [. . .]

if there are any heavens my mother will(all by herself)have one.

—e. e. cummings

MARC CHAGALL *(1887–1985)*

I shall always have a sinking feeling in my heart—is it from sleep or from a sudden memory on the anniversary of her death?—when I visit her grave, the grave of my mother.

I seem to see you, Mama.

You come slowly towards me. So slowly that I want to help you. You smile my smile. Ah! that smile, mine. [. . .]

At the cemetery, at the entrance, I rush forward. Lighter than a flame, than an airy shadow, I hasten to shed tears.

Ah! Mama! [. . .]

I don't ask you to pray for me. You know yourself what sorrows I may have. Tell me, dear mother, from the other world, from Paradise, from the clouds, from wherever you are, does my love console you?

Can my words distill for you a little sweetness, tender and caressing?

—Marc Chagall

EPILOGUE

SAILING HOME FROM RAPALLO

(February 1954)

Your nurse could only speak Italian,
but after twenty minutes I could imagine your final week,
and tears ran down my cheeks. . . .

When I embarked from Italy with my Mother's body,
the whole shoreline of the *Golfo di Genova*
was breaking into fiery flower.
The crazy yellow and azure sea-sleds
blasting like jack-hammers across
the *spumante*-bubbling wake of our liner,
recalled the clashing colors of my Ford.
Mother travelled first-class in the hold;
her *Risorgimento* black and gold casket
was like Napoleon's at the *Invalides*. . . .

While the passengers were tanning
on the Mediterranean in deck-chairs,
our family cemetery in Dunbarton
lay under the White Mountains
in the sub-zero weather.
The graveyard's soil was changing to stone —
so many of its deaths had been midwinter.
Dour and dark against the blinding snowdrifts,
its black brook and fir trunks were as smooth as masts.
A fence of iron spear-hafts
black-bordered its mostly Colonial grave-slates.

The only "unhistoric" soul to come here
was Father, now buried beneath his recent
unweathered pink-veined slice of marble.
Even the Latin of his Lowell motto:
Occasionem cognosce,
seemed too businesslike and pushing here,
where the burning cold illuminated
the hewn inscriptions of Mother's relatives:
twenty or thirty Winslows and Starks.
Frost had given their names a diamond edge. . . .

In the grandiloquent lettering on Mother's coffin,
Lowell had been misspelled *LOVEL.*
The corpse
was wrapped like *panetone* in Italian tinfoil.

                                     —Robert Lowell

FURTHER READING

Joan Acocella. *Mark Morris.* New York: Farrar Straus Giroux, 1993.

Sidney Alexander. *Marc Chagall: An Intimate Biography.* New York: Paragon House, 1978.

Ronald Anderson. *James McNeill Whistler: Beyond the Myth.* New York: Carroll and Graf, 1994.

Isaac Babel. *You Must Know Everything,* with Ilya Ehrenburg's "A Speech at a Moscow Meeting in Honor of Babel, November 11, 1964." New York: Carroll and Graf, 1966.

Philip Callow. *Lost Earth; A Life of Cézanne.* Chicago: Ivan R. Dee, 1995.

Morton N. Cohen. *Lewis Carroll: A Biography.* New York: Alfred A. Knopf, 1995.

Cyril Connolly. *Enemies of Promise and Other Essays.* Garden City, N.Y.: Anchor Books, Doubleday, 1960.

Mary Caroline Crawford. *Goethe and His Women Friends.* Boston: Little, Brown and Co., 1911.

Richard Ellman. *Oscar Wilde.* New York: Vintage Books, a division of Random House, 1987.

Ina Ferris. *William Makepeace Thackeray.* University of Ottawa. Boston: Twayne, 1983.

Wallace Fowlie. *Mid-Century French Poets.* New York: Grove Press, 1955.

G. G. Geller. *Sarah Bernhardt, Divine Eccentric.* New York: Frederick A. Stokes, 1933.

Karen Elizabeth Gordon, *The Ravenous Muse.* New York: Pantheon Books, 1996.

Timothy Hilton. *The Pre-Raphaelites.* New York: Thames and Hudson, 1985.

Michael Holroyd. *Bernard Shaw: A Biography.* New York: Vintage Books, a division of Random House, 1988.

Howard Mumford Jones. *The Harp That Once* (biography of Thomas Moore). New York: Henry Holt & Co., 1937.

Frederick R. Karl. *William Faulkner: American Writer.* New York: Weidenfeld & Nicolson, 1989.

Hugh Kenner. *The Pound Era.* Berkeley: University of California Press, 1971.

Carlton Lake, *Confessions of a Literary Archaeologist.* New York: New Directions, 1990.

Marghanita Laski. *George Eliot and Her World.* London: Thames and Hudson, 1973.

Susan Peck Macdonald. *Anthony Trollope.* University of California, San Diego. Boston: Twayne, 1987.

Gerstle Mack. *Paul Cézanne.* New York: Paragon House, 1989.

———. *Toulouse-Lautrec.* New York: Paragon House, 1989.

André Maurois. *Prometheus: The Life of Balzac.* Translated by Norman Denny. New York: Harper & Row, 1965.

———. *Ariel: The Life of Shelley.* New York: Frederick Ungar , 1924.

Vladimir Nabokov. *Lectures on Russian Literature.* New York: Harcourt Brace Jovanovich, 1981.

———. *Nikolai Gogol.* Norfolk, Connecticut: New Directions, 1944.

George D. Painter. *Proust: The Early Years.* Boston: Little, Brown and Co., 1959.

Enzo Siciliano. *Pasolini.* Translated by John Shepley. New York: Random House, 1982.

Frances Spalding. *Vanessa Bell (1879–1961).* New Haven: Ticknor & Fields, 1983.

————. *British Art Since 1900.* London: Thames and Hudson, 1986.

Henri Troyat. *The Divided Soul: The Life of Gogol.* New York: Minerva Press, 1975.

Martin Van Amerongen. *Wagner: A Case History.* Translated by Stewart Spencer and Dominic Cakebread. New York: George Braziller, 1984.

Helen Vendler. *The Music of What Happens.* Cambridge: Harvard University Press, 1976.

Tennessee Williams. *Twenty-Seven Wagons Full of Cotton and Other Plays.* New York: New Directions, 1945.

William Carlos Williams. *I Wanted to Write a Poem: The Autobiography of the Works of a Poet.* Edited by Edith Heal. New York: New Directions, 1958.

CREDITS

BENJAMIN BRITTEN: Letter from *Letters from a Life: The Selected Letters and Diaries of Benjamin Britten*. Volume I, 1923–1939, edited by Donald Mitchell, University of California Press, 1991. Copyright © 1991 The Trustees of the Britten-Pears Foundation. Reprinted by permission of the Regents of the University of California and the University of California Press.

MIKHAIL BULGAKOV: Letter from *Manuscripts Don't Burn: Mikhail Bulgakov, A Life in Letters and Diaries,* edited by J. A. E. Curtis. Copyright © 1991 by J. A. E. Curtis. Published by The Overlook Press, Lewis Hollow Road, Woodstock, New York, 12498. Used by permission.

PAUL CÉZANNE: Letter from *Paul Cézanne: Letters,* edited by John Rewald and translated from the French by Marguerite Kay, copyright © Sabine Rewald. Published 1941 by Bruno Cassirer, Publishers, Ltd., London. Reprinted with permission of Faber and Faber Limited on behalf of Bruno Cassirer.

MARC CHAGALL: Two quotes and untitled sketch from *Marc Chagall: My Life,* translated from the French by Elisabeth Abbott. Da Capo Press, New York. Copyright © 1960 by Marc Chagall. © 1988 Artists Rights Society, New York / ADAGP, Paris. Reprinted by permission.

JEAN COCTEAU: Letters from *Cocteau: A Biography,* by Francis Steegmuller, Little, Brown & Company. Copyright © 1970 by Francis Steegmuller. Reprinted by permission.

JULIO CORTÁZAR: Excerpt of interview from *Writing at Risk: Interviews in Paris with Uncommon Writers,* by Jason Weiss. Copyright © 1991 by The University of Iowa Press. Reprinted by permission of The University of Iowa Press.

GUSTAVE COURBET: Letters from *Letters of Gustave Courbet,* edited and translated by Petra ten-Doesschate Chu. Copyright © 1992 by The University of Chicago Press. Reprinted by permission of The University of Chicago Press..

E. E. CUMMINGS: Letter and drawing from *Selected Letters of E. E. Cummings,* by F. W. Dupee and George Stade, editors. Copyright © 1969 by the Trustees for the E. E. Cummings Trust. Reprinted by permission of Liveright Publishing Corporation. Line from poem XLIII, *Complete Poems 1904–1962,* edited by George J. Firmage, Liveright Publishing Corporation, New York, copyright © 1991 by the Trustees for the E. E. Cummings Trust.

PHOTOGRAPHS:

Photographs that appear on pages 1, 15, 47, and 139 appear by permission of Alinari/ Art Resource, N.Y.